TELLING

Telling Tails is a personal account of Martin Copland's experience of setting up and running a cat sitting company. The views expressed are those of the author and do not necessarily represent the views of any individuals mentioned in the book. In order to maintain their anonymity in some instances, I have changed some names and places.

TELLING TAILS

The Adventures of a Cat Sitter

Martin
Copland

First published in the UK in 2022
Text © Martin Copland 2022
Design: Word-2-Kindle
Cover illustration:
Word-2-Kindle

The right of Martin Copland to be identified as the author of this work has been asserted by him in accordance with the Copyright Designs and Patents Act 1988.

A CIP catalogue record for this title is available from the British Library.

ISBN: 9798833931578

www.homefuryou.com
FB @HomeFurYou

ABOUT THE AUTHOR

Martin was born in the sixties in Romney Marsh on the East Kent coastline. Growing up, he worked during his holidays on the Romney Hythe and Dymchurch Railway (the world's smallest public railway). He moved to London and ended up working for the Civil Service for over 10 years. But not stuck behind a desk all day in a grey suit, he had the opportunity to travel to the Far East including Jakarta.

After a health scare Martin stepped off the career path and set up a cat sitting business – HomeFurYou. Martin has always owned and loved cats including more recently Posh, Becks and Flo. He now looks after 250 cats in rural Bedfordshire and Buckinghamshire.

Martin has been married three times, (twice to Jules) and they live happily together in a village just outside Bedford.

DEDICATED
TO POSH AND BECKS x

ACKNOWLEDGEMENTS

I have so many people I want to thank, for either inspiring me or helping me along the way. I never expected to be publishing my first book at the age of 60. But I'm glad I finally got it over the line!

First I need to thank my dad. His love of reading and encouraging me to write, has always been a constant in my life. I remember writing a family newspaper at a very young age and inflicting it on my mum, dad and sister. I hope their suffering now seems worthwhile. Thank you to Di Kenny who did the original proofing and to the "Oracle" Katie Wilkins for the final read-through.

The book was mostly written in lockdown in 2020, but the title dated back to the year before. Jules' mum and dad sat down with me in a coffee shop in Warwick and we thrashed out what the book would be called and a rough outline. Thank you both, I hope you love it? The cappuccinos are on me.

I also need to thank my Uncle Michael and Auntie Rosemary here. I can't say why, for fear of ruining the end of the book. But guys - in my mind we made it!!

Not forgetting my amazing cat customers, for providing me with so many adventures both funny and sad.

The book is of course dedicated to the most amazing feline princesses, Posh and Becks. There simply wouldn't be a book without them. Jules and I will always be there for you. You have only brought love into our lives.

We mustn't forget the "Munchkin" Flo, who is responsible for any typos in the book. She loves walking across the computer keyboard.

And last but definitely not least, here's to Holly Willoughby. You'll need to read the book to know why....

But seriously, where would I be without the love of my life. Jules - you are my total inspiration. Thank you for always believing in me and for letting me reach for the stars.

And that's how I feel. You told me I could this. So this one's for you!

Contents

HomeFurYou

PROLOGUE

A catnip mouse at Everest Base Camp

The rainbow coloured prayer flags fluttered in the mountain breeze. We delicately placed the catnip mouse on the snow covered rocks at Everest Base Camp. It was done, we'd fulfilled our mission. The tribute was complete.

You're probably thinking that you've accidently picked up a travel book. But travel is the canvas for this most amazing story, taking you from the slums of Jakarta to the hustle and bustle of New York to the ancient Inca sites in Peru, and many places in between.

You'll find out about the important role that cats have played in my relationships, from my first divorce to "my happy ever after" with Jules.

First there was Snowy, then Michelle, followed by Blackie and Bob – then more recently our precious princesses, Posh and Becks.

Cats have formed such a backdrop to my life that I set up my own cat sitting business. Feeding close to 250 felines really is the best job in the world. Some of the "tails" will make you howl with laughter, whilst others will reduce you to tears.

I'll tell you some ghost stories, many set in our own haunted house. You'll hear about my very short TV career, about pregnant rabbits and why we have a decorated Christmas tree at the bottom of our garden 365 days of the year. You'll also find out why Jules and I celebrate Valentine's Day on 15 February.

Reading this book you may think the "tails" seem rather far-fetched; the reality is every word is true, but obviously some of the names have been changed to protect the guilty and the innocent.

If you're getting over the loss of a beloved four legged friend, then I also hope you'll find some comfort in this book. There is a chapter on bereavement and how to deal with the new norm – life can never be the same, but the memories live on.

So what have cats and mountains got in common - they don't even have cats in Nepal. The answer is simple; we wanted to recognise the life of a very special cat, who touched so many hearts in her lifetime. She is now thankfully at peace.

So in November 2020, we flew to Kathmandu to make this trip of a lifetime. The Covid-19 crisis was behind us, but the world was still recovering from the aftershocks. And this "end of the world" feeling, seemed to add an extra layer of importance to the trip. It seemed to draw a line under so many things. A year best forgotten, but also a year like no other.

A year to remember the love we'd shared with a very special cat during her lifetime.

So yes the book is very much about cats, but it's also about hope for the future. That was exactly the way

Jules and I were feeling at 5,380 metres, up on that cold December day in Nepal.

We raised a glass of the local firewater and our Sherpa guide, joined by our new friends on the tour all took part. Of course, only Jules and I really knew why we were here, but we'd explained to our fellow travellers and they'd embraced the moment enthusiastically.

Jules and I clinked glasses in the cold Himalayan air. The snow-capped mountain on top of the world was our backdrop. We aren't religious (we may be a little bit spiritual), but this felt right. We'd honoured the princess of our hearts, with undying love and affection.

I read out the poem "The Rainbow Bridge" (as I'd done at the graveside) and my fellow travellers burst into spontaneous applause. The deed was done and it felt good.

"We miss you darling". My words were lost in the storm that appeared to be brewing on the mountain high above us. My voice carried on rising until it reached the ceiling of the world.

"Enough, enough now", said Jules and I knew exactly what she meant. We'd done everything for her in life and now in death we'd honoured her.

CHAPTER 1

The lure of the East

My walk to the Embassy took five minutes every morning. This was my time. Time to think, time to reflect on how much I was missing my wife, Clare and my darling ginger tom, Bob.

It was the most colourful, noisy and entertaining commute I'd ever had in my life. Every day was different, every day an adventure.

I walked past schoolchildren who seemed to emerge from riverside slum dwellings every morning. How they looked so smart in their immaculate white shirts I will never know. Their smiles never failed to make my day.

The air was thick with the cinnamon-tipped local Kretek cigarettes and this mixed with the rich aromas rising from the food hawkers stalls. The national dish, Nasi Goreng, was my favourite and I always stopped at one of the cooking stations, to collect my breakfast.

I walked past a local market and marvelled at the amazing variety of fruit – rambutans, durians, papaya and mangosteen…

One of the poorest, most polluted cities on earth was waking up and it was never dull. Jakarta, a city of 16 million people was slowly stretching and yawning its way to a standstill. The traffic gridlock never disappointed; tuk tuks, mopeds and Toyota Kijangs (a family station wagon popular in the region) all slowly ground to a halt.

The humidity was oppressive and by the time I reached the Embassy, I was soaking wet and could have squeezed out my shirt. I never quite adapted to the stifling humidity.

With all this poverty and deprivation around me, I expected the people to be down and depressed, but not a bit of it. I don't think I've ever seen such a happy nation. Maybe if you have nothing, you don't know what you are missing. All I know is that when I left and found myself back in England, I did miss the smiles - especially when travelling on the Underground.

The sights, sounds and colours all around me when I walked anywhere in Jakarta were overwhelming. Some days this could be overpowering, but on others it was life affirming.

This cacophony had been the backdrop to my life for quite a few weeks already, but I still never quite got used to it. There's something about the Far East in the first place that scrambles your brain. From the moment you step out of the airport, it's like being on another planet. I don't have this feeling anywhere else I travel to.

It could just be that the culture and religions are so varied. Whatever it is, I have always loved every minute of it. It never changes, that full assault on all your senses. As I said – another planet.

I was staying at the glamorous Ascott Apartments, slap bang in the middle of the city and just a short 500 yard walk from my place of work – the British Embassy.

I never had to lift a finger in my apartment. A young cleaning maid aged around 16 or so would come in every day and leave the place spotless. This always made me feel guilty, as quite understandably I'd never had servants in my life. As a good working class lefty this really appalled me. He must have earned a pittance and I always tried to engage him in conversation, asking him about his family and his village which was hundreds of miles away. He never once complained about his life and always had a ready smile for me. I learnt so much about the country and its people from him. I found this a humbling experience and looked forward to our conversations.

There was also something symbolic about the sheer height and grandeur of my apartment building. It seemed to me to be some great ivory tower, where I looked down on the poor and dispossessed as they burned tyres for warmth, or tried to beg their way to a meal for the night. I never quite got over some of these feelings. My guilt at my good fortune, outweighing any joy at this opportunity I'd been given.

I was working for the Department of Trade on secondment to the Foreign Office. The six month period seemed short on paper but far too long once I got there.

That evening after work, I ordered an Embassy car. I was on my way to meet some friends for a game of tennis at their apartment block. This was me experiencing the full on life of a diplomat and it didn't always sit comfortably with me. I'd never felt that at ease with privilege and it didn't come more privileged than this. The Embassy staff all had servants in their homes and talked about the locals as if they were second class citizens. When in fact we were guests in their country.

I'd come to Jakarta to try to save my marriage, which in retrospect seems counter-intuitive. Why did I think absence would do the trick? I subconsciously thought this would make us realise what we were missing and pull us together, but of course the opposite was true.

I missed my wife, but I missed my cat even more! Even writing those words now seems strange. But animals are more forgiving of your faults and Bob just loved me for what I was.

I did try to befriend some of the cats in Jakarta, but a lot of them were pretty feral. When you are a cat living in a large dangerous city like this, it really was survival of the fittest. However, there was a regular visitor to the hotel pool every now and again – a mother cat and her two kittens. They seemed quite well fed, probably because they had chosen a five star apartment block in which to hang out, but the strangest thing was the mother's short or stubby tail. I asked one of the barman at the pool why a lot of Indonesian cats seemed to have this. He said that because most people would look after the short tailed variety more, because they believed they were better at catching rats or mice. So natural selection meant this type of cat thrived better.

Talking of the famous Bob (who sadly died in June 2020), I know there have been some very successful books about cats with that name. I've read them and seen the film and got the t-shirt. What a brilliant inspiring story that is too. The fact that a cat can help raise a man who is on his uppers and inspire him to change his life, kick his addiction and get off the streets - gives us all some hope in our darker days. As I write this book, Covid-19 has driven us all back into our homes and the danger is that we risk isolating ourselves and facing our demons without human contact. Our cats and pets are going to be so important to us in these frightening days and months.

The current situation has definitely taken me back 25 years to Jakarta. Thinking about that time now, I may have been suffering mentally when dealing with my new surroundings and my isolation from Clare, Bob, my friends and family. We never gave names to these feelings in those days and men in particular were not very good at airing their state of mind, or need for support. We also lacked social media and even basic emails to stay in touch. Although I think the whole use of smart phones and online contact with people has gone too far, it would have been a lifeline for me at that time.

Animals are just as invaluable as that digital support network in my opinion. They offer a constant source of companionship at all times and seem to have an uncanny sixth sense, whereby they pick up on your moods and comfort you. They can also sense tension and stress in you. In extreme cases, some pets have been able to pick up the fact that its owner may be ill. Truly remarkable in every way.

Which was why I was missing Bob. My Bob was just as handsome and canny as his more famous namesake. Bob was a cool dude.

My wife and I had just moved into a village in Cambridgeshire and although not ready for children yet, thought that we needed a little companion for me, as Clare worked a lot of night shifts as a nurse.

I should just say here that I had met Clare on holiday in Morocco and corny as it sounds, our romance turned into something more serious on our return to the UK. She initially lived in Nottingham and decided to move down to live with me in London. I then got a transfer with my civil service job to Cambridgeshire and we set up home in a beautiful village called Hinxton, south of the city.

Clare eventually trained to be a midwife and I would regularly help her with preparing some of her ante-natal presentations. I got so knowledgeable about this subject, that I'm pretty sure I could have delivered a baby had the need arisen. I remember once watching Euro '96 with some friends round at mine. We saw the match surrounded by posters of a woman's anatomy in quite some detail. I had a fun time trying to explain that one away!

We heard that a small litter of kittens had become available locally through Wood Green (a local animal charity) and trotted over there with the intention of just taking a look, maybe to come away with one, maybe not.

When we arrived, we were greeted with the sight of six adorable felines all competing for our attention. But we only had eyes for one. He looked like a tiger cub. Perfect markings and a boisterous attitude. He just barged to the front and threw himself down at our feet. As I say later in this book, our cats choose us not the other way around.

So with Bob happily in our Renault 5 and nervously watching the scenery whizzing by, we drove him to his new home.

Bob immediately took over the running of the house. We were merely his servants and paying his mortgage. I am sure you are all familiar with this scenario? He slept for the requisite 21 hours a day (cats are really trainee lions) and spread himself out over the bed so that we had little room at all. He hunted like his life depended on it and brought live mice into the house which was always fun. I'm not sure he could understand why we seemed so ungrateful with his regular gifts. He climbed trees, he played rough and basically he just made our lives complete.

He then became the collateral from a broken marriage.

Clare and I had been growing apart for some time and looking back I think that having Bob was a way of trying to make us bond more. However, the constant separations caused by her job and the fact we were sleeping and eating at different times, proved that absence doesn't make the heart grow fonder.

I found out about Clare's infidelity when she came out to join me at the end of my six months in Jakarta. We had always planned a six week trip around the region, at the end of my posting. I noticed that when she came out to see me she seemed strangely distant and knew something was wrong. I couldn't quite put my finger on it until one day in Bangkok; she left a letter out by "accident" while she was taking a shower. It was addressed to our next door neighbour back home. You can guess the rest.

For some reason after this we did complete the holiday, passing through Bali, Lombok and Sulawesi amongst other exotic places. However, I still regret not heading for the airport straight away. Did I really expect to turn it round and how could I trust her going forward? Perhaps I was delaying going home because I knew what I'd have to sort out when I got there?

We came home from Jakarta and Clare basically moved in with the neighbour – this caused quite a stir in the village. Worse still, my rival for her affections also had a cute ginger cat.

Well as if the heartbreak from a broken marriage wasn't enough, the fact that she could switch her affections to Seamus (another ginger tom) so easily, made me even more determined that I would keep custody of Bob.

By the way, it was on one of their weekends away together that I had to try to save Seamus' life. He had received a glancing blow from a car and I rushed him to the vet, but to no avail. My mind was racing from this situation. I imagined them returning and on seeing Seamus carefully laid out in their back garden, that they would see me as some kind of revenge seeking madman. "He killed the cat to get to us!" Nothing could be further from the truth and I breathed a sigh of relief as Clare burst into tears and even hugged me for trying to save his life.

That weekend Clare and I had a kind of truce that seemed like a scene out of the First World War, when the two sides downed weapons and exchanged Christmas gifts. Clare and her new man buried Seamus and even passed me a lager over the fence in appreciation of my trying to save him.

But there was to be no reconciliation.

Clare even saved on removal costs when she moved out and into my love rival's nest. She simply passed her furniture and possessions over the fence! The argument about the CD collection was far more painful to me. Being a lifelong music fan, luring her off the rocky shores of Billy Ocean and towards the Smiths had been an achievement I was very proud of. I think it was when she decided to keep Steve McQueen by Prefab Sprout that made me snap. "It was me that made you cool and a rock chick. All of these CDs should have been mine," I shouted. I'd immediately lost the argument by missing the big picture. Imagine having that kind of argument today in the era of Spotify.

The weird thing when you divorce or split up after a long time relationship, when you've spent all that time thinking about one person day and night, you can see them in the street and basically walk past them as if you'd never known them. This actually happened to me a few years later and I do remember questioning why we had even been together. She seemed like a ghost to me.

And so it came to pass. Bob and I were to live the bachelor life together for a few months. We moved to a nearby village and I decided that cigarettes and alcohol would see me through. For a man well into his 30's I decided that hitting the clubs and bars again would be the best way to sort myself out and meet women. Looking back, I must have been quite embarrassing, but when I repeated the trick nearly ten years after this (details to follow), then that was pitiable.

All through this period, Bob was my rock. He never judged me, certainly not as much as I judged myself and was always there with a happy meow and loud purrs to greet me. This is the thing about cats and animals in general. Unlike people they are never quick to criticise, or do all the things that humans are so adept at. They love you at face value and for the love you give them.

Bob had a lot of love to give and gave it unreservedly. I missed him so much as I drifted off in the back of that Embassy car on those humid Jakarta streets - I became incredibly homesick. My assignment was to last for six months and I felt that this time would rush by.

This was just one month into my time out there and although I loved the job, hosting trade missions for the Department of Trade, it was beginning to seem like a drastic step backwards in my life plan.

Anyway, I duly made it to my game of tennis against some of the Embassy staff. I never enjoyed these as much as the games against some of the local staff I knew. These people knew how to have fun. I often felt I was slightly disapproved of for hanging out with them more, but I hadn't travelled for thousands of miles to spend all my time with Brits.

Even to this day, I shudder thinking about one particular game of tennis I had at my apartment block with these lovely people. It was a very windy day and we were struggling to get a decent game flowing. Just then, we all heard a frightening noise and looked round in horror as metres away an enormous shard of glass fell to earth. Was it from a plane? Were we under attack? It transpired that it had been so windy, that a window pane on the very top floor of the apartment block had blown out of its frame. If I had been a cat, then this definitely would have been one of my nine lives gone.

The months passed slowly and the work kept me going but the weekends could be tough and lonely. I remember one of the highlights being the build up to Burns night in January, when a group of us all learnt Scottish dancing. Now I have two left feet at the best of times, but put me in a kilt and I seemed to turn into some kind of whirling dervish. I impressed even myself but looking back I was just trying to make the best of things and get as much as I could out of the experience.

Another way of escaping was to visit the Embassy beach house just a hundred or so kilometres away or the other house they owned, which was in the nearby hills and surrounded by tea plantations. I found the journeys to these places fascinating. To see extremely poor people scraping a living from the rice paddies or from a small cigarette kiosk was very sobering. The contrast with our own pampered existence has stayed with me and I've never stopped being grateful for my own luck in life.

I spent Christmas and New Year at the latter of these Embassy houses. Thousands of miles away from home, amongst a large group of ex-pats, desperately trying to fit in. They were lovely people and were just trying to help me integrate, but I was missing home and family. I would have exchanged all of this for a hug with my beloved Bob.

As midnight chimed on New Year's Eve, I was dreaming of my tiger cub.

CHAPTER 2

Bob the cat

My new life was up and running and I didn't have a clue what to do with the rest of it. I was back from Jakarta and suddenly thrown into single life in a rented two bedroom house, which was far too near my old house in Hinxton (where my wife and her new lover lived).

Thank God I had Bob. My only connection with my old life, and my partner in crime. I would really recommend a cat if you ever find yourself alone. It's such a positive thing and always gives you a reason to carry on. They depend on you 100% and give so much love in return. But unlike humans, they do this unreservedly and only demand a roof over their head and regular meals. That's the deal, just total devotion. In the midst of me contemplating my mistakes and choices in life, Bob was there to just tell me that everything was going to be just fine. He was right, of course.

So in a strange kind of way, even though I was suffering and in a private hell of sorts, I still felt lucky deep down. I had a good job, some amazing friends and family and I also had the moral high ground. I don't think the last of these should be underestimated.

Everyone was appalled at Clare's behaviour and I don't feel embarrassed for a moment to say I lapped it all up - I needed some positive vibes to carry me forward. I was lucky, people looked out for me. I shall always have the memories of my bachelor life with Bob that was to follow. But his luck wasn't so good early on. He even used up one of his nine lives when he got a large leaf stuck in his trachea. I had no idea what was happening on the day he did it. He came into the house coughing and spluttering and couldn't seem to get his breath. I immediately rushed him to the vets. For all I knew he was dying and seemed in such distress. Surely after all I had been through, I wasn't about to lose my best buddy? Life couldn't be that unfair.

The vets were perplexed and couldn't seem to identify what was causing him such discomfort, so they immediately referred him to a specialist in Kings Lynn of all places. I was so worried that the journey might kill him, but what choice did I have? Like all of my cats, Bob hated travel but didn't utter a murmur the whole journey and I feared losing him on the way. It was the longest hour and a half of my life driving him there. I walked round the town centre for a few hours, trying not to think of what he was going through and fearing the worst.

Several hundred pounds later he was as right as rain, but I do think it weakened him. When he came out of his operation his plaintive cry for food was music to my ears. The size of the leaf was ridiculous. How had he managed to swallow that? Surely I fed him well enough?

We lived perfectly well for a couple of years and Bob always graciously gave up sleeping on my bed when I introduced a few too many women to him during this time. They were short lived relationships and he always gave me that Bob-like knowing look which said, "Dad, you are not ready yet, you are healing, you have me!"

When I least expected it, the love of my life just walked into a room and changed everything. She's still doing that 24 years later.

I was back working in the UK for the Department of Trade and had been promoted to open an office for them at the Business Link in St Albans, offering export support for small businesses. On my return to the UK, a job had come up quite quickly and the whole point of my six month posting abroad had been to get a promotion, so I couldn't miss this opportunity.

The day of the interview came round and I knew my head wasn't in the right place. Clare and I had been arguing about some small detail of our split – probably the CD collection again. I hadn't done enough research for the interview and I felt out of sorts. I came a distant second out of two and totally flunked my promotion. Could life get any worse? The interview had even been with an old Cambridge boss of mine and so I should have been a "shoo in" for the job.

I was quite nervous and lacked confidence in those days and with age comes experience - too young to realise that some days just don't go your way and it's best to just be yourself. For example, years later when I went for an interview, I realised after the first ten minutes this wasn't for me. So I stood up, shook hands with both interviewers and held their gaze as I said, "Now, I don't think this is going well for me or for you, so it's probably best we stop wasting each other's time". The look on their faces was priceless. But it was absolutely the right decision.

Anyway, I digress. Luckily, fate dealt her hand again, because the guy who got the role was from the North East and after a couple of weeks decided not to sign the contract, as he didn't want to move his young family. Suddenly someone up there was batting on my side. Little did I know that this was to be even more fateful, because I would meet my future wife in this role. My boss called me back into the office and I was offered the job - second best, but very happy!

So, I gratefully started the next week and was managing a small team of four. We all met small companies in the area and encouraged them on their first small steps to exporting, usually in Europe.

I'll never forget one incident during this time. A colleague of mine was preparing her research for a meeting with a client who said that they were into welding. Charlotte dutifully got all of the information together and met them at their offices in Suffolk. She seemed a little quiet when she got back and I asked her how it had gone. It transpired that they were a *wedding* company (she had misheard) and she had basically blagged her way through the meeting and used all her knowledge of preparing for her own wedding to get through. We had a lot of laughs at her expense but she took it all in good part.

So back to that woman who changed everything for me. Jules was running a travel company offering itineraries to independent travellers. Her start-up company had had some great success in its first year, even selling some of the guides to British Airways. They now decided to look at how to export them. So on 4 December 1996 (yes I remember the date well), this ambitious businesswoman walked into my offices in St Albans.

I still don't know to this day how I got through the meeting. This vision in a tartan kilt, killer heels and a smile to rival Helen of Troy, had me at "Hello". I'm sure I gave out some vital exporting advice in the meeting, but this was quite difficult, as my chin was on the floor. Some people say they know they have met their life partner or the person they will marry, when they spot them across a crowded room. Well, the room wasn't crowded but it felt like that lightning bolt moment for me.

I then spent the best part of a year trying to engineer a follow-up meeting with Jules and although she met me once more, I did begin to think that I was punching above my weight. She was always polite and always returned my calls, but I never quite got the opportunity I was looking for to ask her out. I decided to revert to my school days and ask a friend to step in and help! Pathetic I know, but it was my last role of the dice. My colleague Wendy had struck up quite a friendship with Jules and they even went out to lunch together sometimes. Well, Wendy had just about had enough of me forever asking her questions about Jules and if she was single or interested in me. So when I suggested that she put in a good word for me, she saw it as a kind of public service. Just to shut me up.

Turns out that Jules had recently split up with her business partner, but thought that I was gay and wouldn't be interested in her! Wendy pretty quickly put her right on that point and I asked Jules out on a date. Apparently she said, "I think Martin is lovely. But I already have far too many gay friends and I'm really looking for a boyfriend!" I was amazed; surely I hadn't talked too much about my love of the Pet Shop Boys to confuse her? The real reason being, that I wore my old wedding ring on my right hand.

Apparently this is a sign of "batting for the other side". I'd just wasted one year of my life when I could have spent it with Jules!

We chose a nice intimate pub in Baldock in Hertfordshire and my abiding memory of that evening is teaching Jules the offside rule for football. Now every man you talk to will tell you that this is sign of true love, so the fact that I was doing this on the first date was a good sign! I laid out the salt and pepper and said things like, "now the defender is the pepper pot – let's call him Tony Adams".

We went on a few more dates and everything started happening so quickly. So by the time I put her company forward for an exporting award, we were an item. The event was to be held at Sopwell House, which is a swanky hotel just outside of London, where the England and Arsenal teams stay before matches.

Jules turned up in an amazing red dress and we checked into the room I had booked for us to stay the night. It cost roughly two months civil servant salary I remember. I'm joking of course, but not by much. The room was amazing with a four poster bed, which to my shame I found myself swinging off in my alcoholic haze - I'd even thought to order champagne for the room. Both of us drank far too much as the evening progressed and I can't remember too much about the ceremony, apart from Jules sitting on my bosses lap and smoking his pipe!

The key moment of the evening arrived and Jules's company duly won their category. She brought the trophy back to our table and I was so proud of her and also my small part in her success.

The rest of the evening was sheer bliss and passed with yet more champagne. We woke in the bar area of the hotel around 2am, blinking into the light as we spied the whole of the Arsenal first team. Surreal! We had some great conversations that night with Arsene Wenger and Marc Overmars amongst others. The latter of which showed quite a bit of interest in Jules. But he was too late. My partner had arrived in my life, and just as importantly, Bob's life.

As the dawn chorus started and we headed for our room, I was amazed to see one of my football heroes had joined us – Tony Adams. I almost held my head in my hands as I heard Jules drunkenly utter the immortal words, "You're pepper pot!" – leaving me to explain what the comment meant.

Jules and I became engaged and then married in two whirlwind years. We shared a house that we bought with the wonderful Bob and all seemed complete. Bob immediately accepted Jules into our lives and in fact they became big friends.

The house was over 100 years old and was one of the original garden city houses in Letchworth in Hertfordshire. We quickly began to discover that it had a past and then things got very interesting and scary. We spoke to a new neighbour of ours shortly after moving in and she told us the history of the house. It seemed that couples and families had never stayed for very long and had either divorced or just moved out in a hurry. The story goes that a married couple lived there 60 years ago and the wife fell down the stairs to her death. The rumour mill started up to the effect that was she was murdered by her husband, as they had a volatile relationship.

Now it turned out that Jules was very spiritual and in the past had seen some ghosts. I believe some people are just more in touch with this kind of thing than others. When she was growing up in Stevenage, aged 10, a man confronted her in her bedroom. Apparently, he just stood there; she froze in terror and looked at the curtains to see if it was the light playing tricks with her eyes. When her dad came up the stairs, the man disappeared. It transpired that no one had ever died in the house, so there was never an explanation.

In the house, I started to witness incidents involving Jules. One night she said that she'd been talking to my granny (who had died two years previously). She described her clothes and her chuckle perfectly and so I really began to believe in something unusual in that house. Another night, I gradually became aware of Jules sitting bolt upright in bed and talking to someone or something. It freaked me out to be honest. Other things started happening, such as music being played upstairs when there was no one in but us. Worst of all, we once walked down to the kitchen in the morning and our knife set was laid out on the floor. Other weird things happened all the time, such as the lights going off and on and the dishwasher starting without us touching it.

At different times, I had friends stay who heard voices in the loft or Jules' dad who asked why there was harp music in the house. We also heard footsteps all the time and even a little girl's shoes were buried in a wall cavity we discovered when we started an extension on the house.

Through all of this, Bob seemed quite disturbed. He would often look past us both at something behind us in the room or whine at an empty space. We became convinced that he could see another person in the house who we couldn't see. Was it the murdered wife who wanted us to find out what really happened?

Clever things, cats. I am sure that they have extra sensory powers and not only can they soothe us and pick up on our moods as I've touched on, but I feel sure they can see the spirit world.

Jules and Bob had a unique relationship. He loved being "roughed up" and played with by Jules, feigning anger and walking out. A couple of minutes later he would be back for more. They were inseparable quite quickly. His beautiful ginger markings made him look like a tiger cub as they fought and I really did think my life was now complete just watching them.

Back to real life. A real life tragedy happened in the house one day. Poor Bob, who was only ten years old and who had been in excellent health, came into our bedroom one morning and flopped down on the floor coughing and in discomfort. Cats can tell you when they need you for sure. We took him to the vets to see what they could do, but unfortunately he had too much fluid on the lungs and we reluctantly decided to spare him from further suffering. Was it the leaf that killed or weakened him? I'll never know for sure, but it may have played a part.

Bob, my companion, my daemon (one for you Philip Pullman fans) had decided that I had found happiness again. My buddy in my dark days was now convinced that I could take it from here. He decided that it was his time to go as I had found love.

We came back from the vets, opened a bottle of brandy, and laid Bob on a garden bench for the day like he was sleeping (we weren't ready to let him go). That night Jules and I buried our beloved Bob, sobbing our hearts out and mourned him for weeks (as we still do). I felt cheated in lots of ways; I thought Bob would be around for far longer than he actually was. Ten years seems so short a life for such a beautiful cat. When I look back on my life, it was one of the hardest times for me and frightening in lots of ways. Jakarta, the end of my marriage and striking out on my own. My loneliness and sense of worth was at low ebb, but Bob sustained me and I wasn't ready to say goodbye.

I'll never forget him and how he helped me through the worst times.

My buddy, my Bob.

CHAPTER 3

When love breaks down

This chapter covers the period just after poor Bob died and shortly before Posh and Becks came into our lives. Jules and I have always had cats in our lives and families. She adored Blackie when she was at school and he used to wait for her to come home each day, waiting at the end of the road. For my part, we had Snowy and Michelle, both loved by my family. Even in the midst of a difficult childhood, when my parents were not getting along, these loving animals brought some peace and joy to our household.

I remember our family Christmases being difficult times, with lots of tears and arguments. As a result of that, my sister and mum have never enjoyed it since. I've gone completely the other way and adore every second – decorating the tree in mid-November and loving every kitsch moment of it. I guess I could have hated it too, but wanted to make up for all those miserable times. It's now my favourite time of year and is associated yet again with a very special cat, but we'll get to that much later on.

Sitting here at the kitchen (the engine room of our house) table writing this book, this chapter has been the most difficult to write. I thought a lot about those cats and more specifically the family dynamics in which they lived. Not all families are perfect (far from it) and there are always two sides to a story, especially when couples split up or marriages go wrong. So, I want to ensure fairness on both sides as a relationship break up is incredibly difficult.

Right now in the era of Covid-19, some families are flourishing and working parents are rediscovering their kids and love of simple pleasures such as walks in the country or playing games. It's almost as if the more innocent times we grew up in have returned. Children are not spending so much time gaming, or on their tablets but actually engaging again with family. The flip side of the coin is of course tragic and quite worrying. Couples trapped in abusive relationships are forced to live together in lockdown and often in small flats with no escape. The true cost of that side of this pandemic will not be known for many years.

So, I've tried not to write this section with rose tinted spectacles, because no one truly knows what goes on behind closed doors. Jules and I were very unhappy for long periods of time, so I will just leave that there and not go into details as they don't matter now. Suffice to say, that Jules is now sitting by my side, drinking a beer and helping me to shape this chapter. Over the coming pages you will find out how this came about and the important role that Posh and Becks have played in our lives. Back to that love of cats as a healing factor again.

So, let's carry on with the story…

The postman arrived and we opened the envelope and signed the Court papers to end our marriage. Jules had popped round to lend me a DVD that I had fancied watching. It was called "Sliding Doors" and starred

Gwyneth Paltrow. If you know anything about the film, you'll know that it's the story of a woman whose life follows two different paths, based on whether she makes it through a closing underground train door or not. The story could almost have been written for us and it has unsurprisingly become one of our favourite movies over the years.

Jules and I were still so in love with each other, but we were following different paths and we wanted different things out of life. As I said earlier, Jules is quite spiritual and years later she told me, that even during those dark days, she had seen a premonition of us together as an elderly couple. In her heart she knew that at some point we might just get back together.

Partly, I think we were on a runaway train that had gotten out of control. Now, we're not saying for one moment that marriage is an institution to take lightly. Far from it, we fought as hard as anyone to make it work.

We were hurtling over the cliff labelled "Do Not Jump" and we didn't have a parachute. Maybe we just had to draw a line under the first marriage and all its mistakes to wipe the slate clean and come back stronger.

Up until to this point, we'd been living separately for two years. We were still very close and we'd do anything for each other and come running at a moment's notice. So why were we in this predicament? I'll try to explain.

So picking up the papers that had arrived that morning, we walked to the Divorce Court in Hitchin together. I know this might seem really strange, but we'd been through all the arguments and upsets by then and we'd formed a really deep bond of friendship. Now, I'm not saying for a moment that sorting out your divorce or even attending court is a trivial matter – far from it. But I guess in our case we had got used to this decision over a couple of years and in that time become good friends. We couldn't live with each other, couldn't live without each other to use another cliché.

I won't linger too long here on how in the short space of four years we had grown apart. There were many reasons and as with all of these things there are two sides to every story. As I am the one writing this book, that wouldn't be fair to Jules anyway. Suffice to say that Jules's jet setting career was hard for us both to handle, because absence doesn't always make the heart grow fonder. I remember so many occasions when I had to take her to the airport on a Sunday morning and the rest of the weekend seeming to stretch out for ever. I would never criticise her doing this either, because her job's enabled us to have a very comfortable life.

It was just that we often became "ships that passed in the night". I'd spend the week living effectively a bachelor life and when she arrived home on a Friday, I'd get annoyed about trivial things such as why she'd left her suitcases in the hall or just dumped her whole weeks dirty washing in a heap. Just stuff that didn't actually matter.

So if we were such friends by the time we reached Hitchin Court, what had gone wrong in our marriage to make us come to our fateful decision? Personally I think it was just bad timing on my side. I had fallen in love with Jules too quickly after the end of my first marriage and I guess I just wasn't ready for that commitment. Jules for her part was probably driven very much by the career path and perhaps if that hadn't entailed so many trips abroad, we could have made it work?

During our first marriage we always had Bob around as you have read. He was from a broken home of his own when I was married to Clare and so he'd adapted to different situations so well. He went from married home to broken home, to married home and back again to single. He never complained or looked unhappy as he was moved from house to house. Jules grew to love Bob during our marriage and was there when he sadly passed away. So cats have always featured heavily in our time together.

Before I moved out, my stuff was all piled up in the lounge of our house in Letchworth - I was waiting for my house purchase to happen. We were living in the same house but leading separate lives, so it was very difficult for us both. Passing the piles of furniture and belongings in there, day after day was difficult for both of us and a physical reminder of what was to come. Jules told me years later that she found this almost unbearable each day and used to cry on the way to work in London. But we both held it together in our jobs each day and never took a day off sick during this time.

We never talked about it to colleagues either, believing that the stiff upper lip was the way to go. Perhaps this was the wrong approach and 24 years later, it seems strange to say that, when everyone is much more in touch with their feelings. Mental illness is not a taboo.

Jules has often told me that the way she coped during those times, was to drift off to a "rustic green table in a French vineyard". We are both seated at the table drinking wine and talking about our lives and saying, "What was that all about?" Whenever life gets tough, Jules takes herself to that place.

One difference from my divorce with Clare was that we didn't have to argue over the CD collection this time! Jules let me have the lot as her taste in those days amounted to Lionel Ritchie and Barry Manilow. It was only years later that I turned her into a cool rock chick. We did split all the family appliances though, so I ended up with a dishwasher and a washing machine, she had the microwave and the cooker. Amazing how white goods become bargaining tools!

Eventually my completion date arrived and I moved out to my own house in Eaton Socon (in Cambridgeshire) and Jules and I stayed in touch. If ever either of us was in trouble or needed something, the other one was always there.

All the signs were there in the four years that we were apart - we had made a terrible mistake. It was just that we both needed to do some growing up to realise that mistake. Some of that growing up included meeting several new partners and trying to convince ourselves we had found "the one".

Back at the court in Hitchin, we waited our turn by sitting in the waiting room. We were the only couple in there and found ourselves surrounded by lawyers and sad looking individuals. We simply went to see the official, signed our names and the deed was done. No recriminations, no bitterness. It wasn't our time to be together.

Fast forward to 8 May 2020. Jules and I were cycling through Hitchin on the 75th anniversary of VE Day in the middle of the Covid-19 lockdown. So many of these memories came flooding back. It was a strange day, with people social distancing and friends talking to each other over the garden gate. But it was life affirming and reminded me that after the lack of community spirit since the Brexit vote and the divisions of the last few years, that this country was able to pull together again in adversity. It also reminded me that in 2003, Jules and I walked up to a court house in the same town and we signed a piece of paperwork. It could have been the finish of things for us, but it turned out to be a necessary pause for us to start up our relationship later on. That way we were able to rid ourselves of any baggage and start afresh with our love affair.

On this day, it seemed appropriate to remember that we'd said "We'll meet again" all those years ago and perhaps we even knew then that our story would also have a happy ending.

Vera Lynn would have been proud of me!

CHAPTER 4

The girls chose us

The two black and white kittens yawned and stretched as they woke up with their siblings, on a cold morning in springtime. They looked around their surroundings and immediately cried out for their mother. Where had she gone and why had she abandoned them? Only yesterday they had been feeding with her and playing and fighting with each other and the world had seemed a safe place.

Now they seemed to be in an old fruit box and in someone's front garden. Mum was nowhere to be seen, but a friendly looking humanoid was coming down the garden path to greet them. "Oh bless you guys! Who could have abandoned you like this?" But to be honest Mrs Smith had seen this time and time again. Why did people keep animals and then decide they could no longer afford to keep them or just abandon them. At least this owner had chosen the garden of a Cats Protection safe house in which to leave them.

Cats Protection has been caring for the nation's cats in need for over 90 years now. Cats in the UK have been on quite a journey ever since 1927 when the League was set up. They were not considered to be the wonderful companions we think of today, in fact a lot of people used to think of them as pests, hence the forming of an association to look after their interests. Their next big test was during the Second World War when the Blitz was at its height, particularly in London. The Cats Protection League again came to their rescue as lots of cats were displaced by the bombing and lost their owners or became strays. The League set up a "Tailwavers" scheme to relieve the suffering of our feline population.

More recently Cats Protection have encouraged the micro chipping and neutering of cats to control their population. They now have thousands of volunteers working for them and a similar number of supporters who finance their good works.

So the cute black and white kittens waking up in a fruit box had certainly chosen the right house to be abandoned at. Meanwhile somewhere in Hertfordshire, Jules' nieces had built up a strong relationship with me and she wanted them to stay in touch. The nieces were both very young at the time and so didn't really understand the break up.

What to do to keep a connection between all of us? Well I'd always wanted cats and badly missed my ginger tom – Bob. As you know, he had recently died after helping me through some tough times after the end of my first marriage. The perfect answer for all seemed to be for me to get a cat.

Jules had contacted Cats Protection and heard that they might have some kittens for us to see. I was really keen on another boy cat, so went along with that thought.

The minute we walked in Mrs Smith's living room, we fell in love about eight times over. There were kittens of all types. There were ginger ones, there were grey ones and there were two adorable black and white ones. Well to be honest, one was mostly black with white markings and the other was almost like the negative image of that.

We chose them or should I say they chose us. This is always the way as anyone in this situation will tell you. The others didn't stand a chance as the two kittens sidled up to us and started playing. When we then heard that they were sisters and had been abandoned together, we couldn't part them. Following the usual checks and home visit from Cats Protection, we finally got the green light to pick up the girls.

As soon as we got the girls home to my recently bought pad in Eaton Socon, the nieces demanded to see them, so that part of the deal was already working. We gave them complete naming rights and suggested that they would be the "godmothers" of one each. So it was a very close run thing that they were almost called Buffy and Angel. Younger readers may wish to check out a series called Buffy the Teenage Vampire – a 90's classic.

Luckily a film which had appealed to a lot of young girls at the time had just come out. "Bend it like Beckham" had featured a young Keera Knightley who wanted to make it in girl's football and idolised David Beckham (as did I). So naturally the girls were named Posh and Becks.

The house in Eaton Socon was full of character and a short walk from the River Ouse. There were lots of green spaces and walks around the area. I was very lucky in my job at the time, because I could basically choose to live anywhere in the East Anglian region. My role as a Regional Manager covered the whole of the area from Lowestoft in the east, to Watford in the west. I was a bit nervous about choosing the house on my own, so Jules kindly agreed to come along. We spent weekend after weekend looking for the right house in the right area. I was looking after the East Midlands area for a colleague on long term sick leave. I even put an offer in on a house in Matlock, before I got cold feet about being so far apart from Jules.

So eventually I chose Eaton Socon. The "girls" (they will always be known as "the girls") lived with me for a couple of years and Jules was a regular visitor. I truly believe they were the glue that kept us together. We exchanged notes and calls about our lives and relationships, we hung out with the girls, we laughed, we talked. Gradually the visits got longer and the connection deeper. No one else came close.

One evening we'd bought tickets to see Lionel Ritchie (one of Jules' favourites) at Wembley Arena and we took her sister Sue along. I felt for Sue every time Lionel wheeled his piano on stage and played one of the more soppy romantic songs. Jules and I just went all gooey and had tears in our eyes, even though we were just friends by this time. Another sign that we would be together in the future?

Posh and Becks loved having Jules around even though we were just friends. Becks, in particular, has always been a friendly cat with new people, but Posh has an otherworldliness about her which can be unnerving.

One morning, after a visit the night before by Jules, Posh looked at me from her usual resting place on the bed. She almost seemed to be saying that Jules and I had deviated from our plans that had been laid out for us. It depends if you believe in life being mapped out from the day you are born, or is it haphazard? We believe the former. We'd always credited Posh with human feelings and thoughts. There was just something in those eyes that seemed all knowing. Something about the way she looked into your soul. I think she'd been reincarnated from human to cat. I quite fancy making the journey the other way round when I move on - what a life that would be. To be honest though it would have to be in a house like ours, where you get waited on hand and foot and you are spoilt rotten. Posh's look that morning was one of exasperation and something else. What was that something else?

Jules even did some pretty extensive redecorating works on my house in Eaton Socon in between her glamorous overseas trips and boyfriends. For my part, I was meeting several different women, but no one that lit that candle. There was one who had a cat, so that appealed. Now this cat only had three legs, so my friends took great delight in calling her the "Three legged cat woman!"

I felt like I was losing Jules but wished her well in her exciting life. Not realising that she was quite unhappy and lonely and was actually being drawn back to me. For my part, I decided that for the second time in my life, I needed to drink, smoke and go to clubs (with my friend Mark), but we were far too old. I was repeating the mistakes from the end of my first marriage, and with age and experience I should have known better.

I shudder to think what I put Bob and then Posh and Becks, through by introducing them to several new people. Now I know what it must be like to get your children to like their new step mother or father. I for one should remember what that felt like, because my Mum divorced my Dad and married my Headmaster at secondary school. I didn't hang around at school much after that, as you can imagine.

The girls loved the house in Eaton Socon. My abiding memory of them is that I would sometimes lamely try to go jogging (never my strongpoint), in the adjacent park that I could see from my house. The kittens would outrun me into the park every time. Happy days.

Another funny incident comes to mind. I had a bath there but no shower, so every night I'd take a bath, drink wine and read a book. Both girls always joined me in there and Posh even got brave one night and jumped onto the side of the bath, only to slip right in under the soap suds! I'll never forget her poor bedraggled face as she gasped for air before I pulled her out. These were great bonding days with them, great for my mental health and helped to combat my loneliness at the time.

I then moved myself and the girls to a new housing development called Cambourne in Cambridgeshire. I felt it would have more for a single man to do. There was a pub, tennis courts and a large supermarket - I felt I would have more of a social life there. The girls were happy in this new house, despite living next to Max the dog and a couple of cats. Becks always made me laugh during these times. She'd sneak into the neighbour's house, steal the dog's toys and pile them up in my sitting room. She would also hang out with this Max and I remember vividly the day my neighbour quickly beckoned me round, to see Becks and Max cuddled up together in front of the fire like they were best buddies.

It was Posh who once caused me to have palpitations; in fact I thought I'd lost her. Both girls came and went freely as they had a cat flap and would often roam over quite a distance in the neighbourhood. There were even some days when I didn't see one or the other for a day or so, but I never worried too much because they always came back and it was a quiet, safe road.

Then one day, Posh went missing for a couple of days and I did begin to think this was quite odd. When it got to two days and then three, I was seriously concerned. Jules was flying back from South Africa that morning after another exciting business trip. As usual she rang me to ask how I was doing. I remember being so upset and blurting out that I thought Posh must have got run over. I distinctly remember Becks pining for her, even though most of the time they just ignored each other and led very separate lives.

Jules came straight over with two large takeaway coffees, mostly for her to ward off the effects of jetlag. We always did this for each other. We were always there for each other. I remember combing pretty much the whole of Cambourne. We must have walked for miles as it had grown to literally thousands of homes by that time. Still nothing. We put posters up with Posh's picture on them and offered a reward.

A week went by and I was heartbroken. I felt I'd lost her. Had she got run over and just been left at the roadside? Had she strayed too far and got lost? Unlikely, because most cats know their "patch".

Jules had been searching with me every night. I imagine her boyfriend at the time was overjoyed about that! She then needed to go on another of her business trips, so I carried on alone.

Two weeks had now gone by. I even got to thinking about maybe making a memorial to her - I was so certain she had disappeared. I sat in the front garden. It was the middle of a heat wave in July. Becks nuzzled up to me without a care in the world and I actually cried.

Becks without Posh, it was like Bonnie without Clyde, Corbett without Barker or Lennon without McCartney. I sipped my mid-morning coffee and then there she was!

POSH!

She looked half the cat she used to be as she had lost so much weight, but it was definitely Posh. She meowed to say hello and then walked calmly into the kitchen and promptly ate two bowls of food like nothing had happened.

I can only think that she had wandered into someone's shed or summer house a couple of weeks before and then got locked in. Perhaps the owner had then gone on holiday for two weeks and only let her out on their return?

I should of course have taken her to the vets there and then, as she looked so malnourished. But she made such a quick recovery and gained weight in just a week, so no serious damage was done.

I was overjoyed and called Jules before anyone else. That should have told me something in itself. She had just returned from her trip and rushed over to see the girls. We celebrated together and I made dinner for the four of us.

And then - Jules and I fell in love all over again. I'll tell you more about that later on in this book as that one deserves its own chapter!

The nieces by the way lost any interest in them when they discovered music and Brandon Flowers from the Killers. But we give them enough love, as if we are their real mum and dad.

We never had kids, so they are our family.

CHAPTER 5

Houston we have a problem

The year is 2005 and I'm in Lima, Peru. Hardly the most glamorous place in the world. Its grey, concrete, featureless landscape was pretty bleak. But what had happened before would stay with me forever. We had been trekking for 10 days in the most stunning Peruvian countryside. We had seen ice blue lakes, lush jungle landscapes and of course, the piece de resistance; Machu Picchu.

I was sharing this trip with 39 other likeminded souls, two tour guides and a team of amazing sherpas who did all the hard work for us. Every day they cooked us breakfast, lunch and dinner, took down the camp and transported it all by mule and then set up camp again for the next evening.

We all had our reasons for taking part in the trek and the charity we raised funds for was very worthy – Mind UK (a mental health charity). However, I also had my own personal reasons for taking part and these were based around the aimless life I was leading since splitting up with Jules. I had plenty of friends, a lovely house in Cambridgeshire and best of all Posh and Becks, who never failed to cheer me up. Even my job was great.

But something was missing - it was Jules. She'd met an American guy (we'll call him the Cowboy to protect his feelings) and had decided to get engaged and go out to Houston to live with him. They'd even started to look for houses together. I guess I knew this was the end of the road for us and that she would not be coming back again. In my heart I'd never given up on reconciliation, but this was the final nail in my heart. We were still brilliant friends and stayed in touch, but now with the Atlantic between us that was becoming less frequent.

So flying to Peru was my own way of drawing a line under everything. I would need to grow up, stop hitting the clubs (especially at my age) and try and make something of my life. Marriage was certainly not on the radar as I had proved how bad I was at that. I was ready for a relationship and so given that my job introduced me to an almost totally male population, I decided to try internet dating. This was years before the convenience of swiping right of course! Some of the girls I met were lovely and great company, but I couldn't help comparing them with Jules, so I tended to make excuses and get out of the second dates.

Then I heard about an exciting new concept called speed dating. This must have been one of the quickest fads to rise and fall in those days, but for a very short while it was *the* way you got into relationships. Basically, you walked into a pub or club in the evening and there were around 20 men and the same number of women in the room.

A whistle was blown and you had three minutes to meet a woman who came to your table, ask her questions, get asked some of your own and try to work out if you wanted to see them again. Not exactly deep and meaningful.

I managed to get a few relationships to a second date this way and some of them definitely had potential, but again I felt the timing wasn't right.

Jules also had a couple of relationships during this time and I remember one very scary situation that arose out of one of them. She'd gone to Oman with this particular guy and all seemed to be progressing well. She'd just passed her PADI diving qualification and so Oman was a good location to try this out. The trip seemed to be going OK until they went to try out a shipwreck dive. It seems like the organisers were not the safest company in the world and her "buddy" took her down to over 30 metres and then into the shipwreck, sometimes in complete darkness.

Cue a very scared Jules - when she came up, she didn't talk to anyone for two hours. She suffered severe ear damage from not equalising and was very angry with the organisers for getting her into the situation. She later reported the diving company to PADI, who took the accusations very seriously. So who did she call to let off steam about this? Well me, of course. I happened to be wasting money of my own in the same timezone and was on a five day luxury holiday to Dubai. I have no idea what made me book this but I felt it would cheer me up!

I distinctly remember being in the middle of some retail therapy when I got the call on my mobile. Jules was literally sobbing down the phone and telling me about the diving accident. It seemed like she had been very lucky not to be more seriously injured or even dead.

Very much like a cat, Jules seems to have had more than her fair share of "nine lives" moments. She very nearly got caught up in the 7/7 bombs on the London Underground and she was also near to the scene when fire destroyed part of Kings Cross station in 1987 and killed many people. She has also had bad skiing accidents and other near misses too numerous to mention – her parents would kill me if they knew.

So I was very concerned when she called me from her diving holiday, but also intrigued that she had chosen to call me to vent about everything. Perhaps there was some hope after all?

That hope was dashed soon afterwards when she started dating the Cowboy and planning her move to the States. Her company, Shell, paid for the relocation and she was offered a three year contract in Houston.

Jules did a lovely thing before she left for the States. She took me out for dinner and then came back to mine to hang out with Posh and Becks. We played with them all evening and she even stayed in the spare bedroom where Posh snuggled up to her all night. They were very close and we do credit Posh with human feelings and senses. I do wonder if Posh knew what was happening that night as Jules held her close. Or perhaps Posh was the really clever one and could see the depth of love that was still there between Jules and me. Did she know this was just a hiatus and not the end of us?

The next morning I waved Jules off and thought that would be the last time I would see her. I held it together until the moment the door closed and then sobbed my heart out. It was only after a couple of strong coffees and some moping around for an hour or two that my eye caught the 'Mind Peru' leaflet which had dropped out of the Guardian. (I was an annoying lefty even back then).

"Trek Peru and see the amazing ancient Inca site Machu Picchu" it screamed at me in bold letters. But what I actually read was "Get over Jules and try and get yourself a life - you waster!"

I was always very harsh on myself in those days, but knew for sure that I needed to stop trading on past glories. If Jules was out of sight and we weren't meeting up, surely this would get easier. So I did a positive thing to begin my new life – I booked that trip.

I wasn't the fittest in those days, so I planned a couple of visits to Derbyshire to do some walking. I bought all the trekking kit and I read up on the Incas and bought the Peru guide. I also did some car boot fairs to raise some of the sponsorship money, having almost left myself broke travelling to Dubai.

In those days, we didn't have smartphones and made calls very sparingly - especially if we were abroad. So I didn't hear a lot from Jules and totally understood that. When we did talk, it seemed to be going well. The Cowboy was very religious which I think would have been hard for her to understand as we were both committed atheists! But god moves in mysterious ways I believe.

Anyway, I had wished her all the best for the future before she packed her bags for Houston and sincerely wanted it to work out for her.

That whole sentence is a lie.

I couldn't bear it. But I was proud of myself for trying to move forward and do something positive. I am a "glass half full" bloke on the whole and I was young enough to think there would be a third chance at happiness somewhere out there. Despite which, Posh and

Becks had come from a broken home and needed to have a stepmother at some point.

I attended the briefing in London the month before we were due to fly. We met at the MIND offices and were greeted by one of the ladies who was to be our tour guide. She was a bundle of energy and the group consisted of pretty similar ages to me on the whole, so that was a big plus. I'm not a natural in a big crowd, but figured that I could blend in with this group - and maybe find one or two people with similar interests. This would be fun and I came away thinking, "roll on Peru".

I did speak to Jules a couple of times before I left for Peru, but she seemed a little distant and even a little down. I think there were some big steps to overcome like settling down in a new country and having to meet his kids. Having never wanted children of her own I'm sure she found that one a bit strange.

So, it didn't even occur to me that her new life was struggling to take-off and in my mind it was all going swimmingly.

Arriving at Heathrow felt scary and exciting all wrapped up into one - meeting 39 strangers was good for me. A bit like one of those speed dates I mentioned earlier, as we all jockeyed for who we wanted to sit next to on the plane. I managed to choose a lovely blonde girl I had met at the briefing in London. I must have known I was going to carry on being irresponsible in matters of the heart, because I never go for blondes. Anyway we struck up a nice conversation and the time certainly rushed by, helped by the several glasses of red wine we managed to squirrel out of the flight attendants. I knew this wouldn't end well but I was enjoying myself again for the first time in months.

We arrived in Lima, the capital of Peru and then got a transfer to Cusco to start our acclimatisation. Bizarrely, two of the people in our tour promptly fainted as soon as we got into the airport. One even crashing into a pain of glass. The altitude is only 3,400 metres but there is no telling how this will affect your body. Fitness or weight doesn't come into and no one can really prepare properly. All I knew was that it didn't bode well for the rest of the hike which took in altitudes of up to 4,200 metres.

We spent a couple of days getting used to this in Cusco and it was fantastic. Very Spanish in feel, a lot of us basically just hung around the coffee shops, doing a little bit of sightseeing. It was during these early days that we began to develop a taste for cocoa leaf tea. An amazing concoction which I think probably had some drug like properties, but only in mild form. It certainly made us relax and even seemed to help with the altitude sickness. During these few days and the entire trek, it seemed to me that although people were pairing and grouping up with likeminded souls, everyone was being very respectful to each other and just having some innocent fun. That certainly changed at the end of the hike!

10 days later, with Machu Picchu successfully mastered and after spending nine nights in freezing cold temperatures in tents, it was like the safety catch had been removed. We all went out to a couple of clubs back in Cusco and I've never seen a scene like it. Couples were pairing off all over the place and roommates politely asked if they wouldn't mind switching rooms for the night. It was like a scene from the Roman Empire. I had no idea what unleashed this orgy of misbehaviour, but I was hardly complaining. I remember my workmates asking me on

my return about how I had managed this at altitude but I was acclimatised by then!

Cue a lot of red faces on the way back to Heathrow a couple of days later and even some distancing as some people arrived back to be greeted by partners, husbands and wives. It was like I was given a tiny taste of what the sixties must have felt like. I always thought I had missed out by being born ten years too late!

Meanwhile – somewhere in Houston, we had a problem

Jules was having a torrid time. The Cowboy had begun to feel uneasy about their relationship and probably influenced by a higher power – his god – decided that he should do the decent thing and go back to his wife and kids with his tail between his legs. Amazing that he hadn't worked this one out before making Jules move her life thousands of miles away and her believing in this so much that they got engaged. God moves in mysterious ways, as I've said.

So, there I was at Heathrow. I was wearing my walking boots (easier than packing them) literally covered in Peruvian mud. As soon as I turned on my mobile and supped a first Costa in two weeks, I got a call. It was Jules and she sounded upset.

I asked her what was wrong and between tears she poured out the whole story. It sounded terrible and she felt like she had been abandoned miles from home, locked into a three year contract with Shell. She sounded so lost and like a little girl. I asked her if she had called her mum and dad, but she said that I was the first person she had called. I found this amazing. We had always been there for each other through the good and bad times. We'd always reached out to each other, but I thought that had gone when she moved to the States.

I told her that she didn't need to stay out there and that I'd be on the first plane out to see her and I knew her mum would feel the same. Strangely this wasn't the moment when I knew that I would always be with her, that was still to come. But let's face it, the signs were there.

A week later I left Gatwick airport not really knowing how I could help, but so looking forward to seeing Jules. She picked me up at George Bush International Airport. For the following week I just tried to give her a great time and we hung out as much as we could around her work commitments. We didn't start our relationship up again at this point, we just talked and talked. I told her that Posh and Becks were doing just fine and would love to see her again if she decided to come home. Of course she was still upset about the break-up she'd been through and she still had feelings for him. I think in her heart she knew that relationship was over. So I tried to just be there for her in every sense of the word.

I think she'd already decided that she would approach Shell to see if she could switch her contract back to the UK, but that was going to take a few weeks if not months. Her mum had promised to come out and help her pack when the time came, but in the meantime it was great just to be together.

She had become quite the expert driver in Houston. But it was our trips out of Houston to Galveston and to San Antonio that we really loved. Leaving behind such an unloved city for these romantic getaways was bliss and just what Jules needed.

The day came for her to drive me back to the airport. I needed to get back home because I had basically used up most of my annual leave in around four weeks!

I'll get to the end of the story I promise, but there was just one very strange thing that happened to us on the way to the airport. Both of us experienced a very weird feeling in the car, as if we had lost some time. We both seemed to lose consciousness and be much further along the road with around 20 minutes of time having elapsed. Were we abducted by aliens, did we bend the space/time continuum? We both felt it and we talked about this years later. What had happened? Had we been taken over by aliens? Maybe it was just our body clocks clicking back into symmetry with each other. Maybe the next part happened because of that?

I remember the airport perimeter fence coming into view and I sensed that we were tensing up as a result. I didn't want to leave Jules, but if I had to leave her now, I knew I had to tell her how I felt about her. Remarkably Jules was feeling the same way as me, but didn't know how to articulate it either.

I saw the lights of planes taking off and landing in the early evening haze of pollution. A song had been on my mind for about a week, now having just been released - Fix You by Coldplay. One of the lyrics came into my head as I watched the lights of the plane as we headed back to the UK.

"Lights will guide you home
And ignite your bones
And I will try to fix you"

I knew it in that moment. As Jules dropped me at the kerb, I let out the most incoherent sobbing as did she. All the words I had practiced on that journey were forgotten. I was annoyed with myself. But somehow this great release of emotion on both our parts got the message home.

Jules was coming home to Posh and Becks.

This time it was for keeps.

CHAPTER 6

Lucky in love

When the plane landed back at Gatwick I'd spent the whole flight thinking through my future with Jules. The fact that we had sobbed our hearts out, made me certain that this time it was for ever. I hoped that in her apartment in Houston, she was thinking the same way. If my life ever had a pivotal moment, then the scene at George Bush International was it.

When the plane landed at Gatwick, I headed for Costa and ordered a large cappuccino. This was followed by a wonderful life affirming call with Jules on my way home and I felt about ten feet tall as I spoke to my next door neighbour in Cambourne – Jan. She reassured me that Posh and Becks had been having sleepovers with Max and were in fine fettle. When you're away from home it's always nice to know that someone responsible is looking after your cats.

We'll return to that theme later on!

I arrived back in Cambridgeshire and thought about how my life would be changing. I didn't think for a moment that this wouldn't work out, we were just so sure of what we would do. Of course I had to have a chat with Posh and Becks and explain the situation. They took it very well and were excited that the family would be back together again.

There were still a lot of things for us to put in place before we could get back together. Jules needed to come back for a start and this entailed asking her company for a role back in the UK. She then needed to explain to her landlord that she didn't want to go on renting and ending the lease agreement on the hire car. None of this was a problem though, compared to telling friends and family that we'd be getting back together again. We decided not to do that, until we were 100% certain that we would live together.

Even close family members, and our best friends, were kept in the dark for a period of around 12 months. The only exception was Jules' parents because we'd asked her mum to go out to Houston and help pack Jules' flat up. They were cool about it all, but we knew others wouldn't understand as easily. When couples split up, it's easy for friends to take sides. Then when you get back together again, it's hard not to remember what they said in the heat of the moment. You end up really knowing your real friends, which is fairly positive anyway.

One of the funny things about this time, was that Jules had to send her belongings back to the UK by sea. It took months, so she was left pretty much with the clothes she stood up in. In fact her stuff was at sea longer than she'd been in Houston.

I'd waved goodbye to Jules in the June of 2005 and didn't see her again until August, when she came back for good.

Even then we kept living in our old houses, Jules in Letchworth and me in Cambourne. We dated in secret for around six months and it was just like the first time, but in some ways more exciting. We had to "wrap" the old arguments in a big box and bury them forever or at least that's the way we visualised it. It worked, we treated it like a new relationship with all the excitement, date nights and wooing that happened first time round. Best of all, this time Posh and Becks were there to enjoy it. The good vibes in the house flowed directly into them and they seemed so happy as a result. I've touched several times on the calming influence cats can have on humanoids, but we were repaying the debt this time around.

They showed how happy they were by spreading themselves across our bed. We just about managed to arrange ourselves around them and then they started to stretch out. I found myself one side of the bed and Jules was on the other. One memorable night after attempting one too many contortions to fit round them, I remember saying to Jules that we should leave them to it. We literally got up in the middle of the night and walked off to the spare bedroom! Who says cats are masters of the house and we are the servants?

All was going swimmingly in both our human relationship and with our feline family. After a couple of months, we both felt confident enough for me to sell my house and move back in with Jules. I got a buyer really quickly and we thought that this would happen without a hitch, but with just a couple of weeks to go the buyer pulled out. Was this an omen? Were we to be unlucky in love once again, were we jinxed?

Luckily we weren't, because in a buoyant market I got another buyer really quickly and the sale proceeded at speed. We had our date for me moving back in. Posh and

Becks would be back where they belonged – in the heart of a loving family.

For the last time in their lives, they would leave behind a broken home. They were on their way back to their mum and to a loving environment again. I packed the car and then handed over the car keys to Jules who carefully belted the girls in to the back seats. I climbed into the hire van and we left Cambourne for good, back to our home in Letchworth. It was sunny; the girls were wide eyed at the glimpses of hedgerows and a little scared of the traffic all around them. They don't even like a short visit to the vet so the thought of a trip of 30 odd miles wasn't making them relax. But Jules put the radio on for them and whispered sweetly about their life to come.

Letchworth had been our marital home and we'd always loved it there. There were problems of course between Jules and me the first time around. But an even stronger feeling lingered, that perhaps the house was the problem back then. There has always been a high turnover of owners in the house and a fair share of divorces or splits. Had the spirits moved on? The house had a different feel to it, maybe the ghosts had moved on? For some reason, my coming back home must have squared the haunted circle, because we didn't ever experience the same thing again. Posh and Becks were never disturbed by strange forces as Bob was and Jules never again felt any presence or spirit life.

Of course, as we had now moved in together, we had to tell all of our friends and family. They took it well on the whole and were really behind us. We've since discovered that getting back together and remarrying (as we would do later) was far more common than we ever thought it was. Of course one of the most famous couples to remarry, actually did this too! Elizabeth Taylor and Richard Burton were a hard act to follow, but we gave them a run for their money.

Meanwhile in the feline world, the girls were exploring the bigger garden they had now been presented with. They were incredibly streetwise as we lived on a main road. I don't know why some cats are better at this than others at this, but we have always been lucky in this regard with our cats. Maybe one of them had a narrow escape one day and learned their lesson or perhaps some cats are just less adventurous?

The other weird novelty for Posh and Becks was black squirrels. Now this was a phenomenon I'd never come across before either. When I saw my first one, I thought it must have been a grey squirrel which had fallen in bucket of tar. The real story is a little more complicated. Apparently they are derived from a rare mutation of grey squirrels and fox squirrels. They can be found mostly in the USA but there is quite a concentration of them in the South East of England, especially Stevenage, Hitchin and Letchworth. The other theory is that they started as zoo escapees from nearby Woburn Abbey and have just bred and bred in large numbers.

Posh and Becks were freaked out. They never managed to catch one, (even in their younger days), but they certainly gave it their best shot.

The girls loved the house and garden and they roamed it freely and safely. The next door neighbour owned a very cheeky ginger tom cat called Seamus. In the summer, he would creep up on the unsuspecting Becks as she slept in the sun and very gingerly (excuse the pun) tap her on the back before disappearing into the undergrowth. She never spotted where her attacker had come from or who he was.

We had another three wonderful years in our Letchworth home. We'd seen off a ghost, fallen in love for the second time and given our family (Posh and Becks) all the love they deserved. What could possibly go wrong?

In 2008, there was the biggest banking crash since the 1930s and it was truly global in scale. It's ironic that I'm writing this book in a time when those previous two crashes will be cast into the shadows. Not by banking failure and human error, but by a pandemic which has affected every country in the world. The damage we're now going through will cast its shadow for generations to come. It will affect the economy, the jobs market and people's mental health. I'll write far more about living through this time later and will focus on some of the more positive aspects, such as the sense of community and the solace our pets can give us in time such as these.

Back in 2008, it was enough that it caused unemployment and the housing market to collapse. The latter of these affected us more than anything, just at the time we wanted to move house.

We had spent over ten years in Letchworth in our beautiful Garden City property. We thought that it must have really increased in value, to enable us to follow our dream and move to the country. As an original Garden City house it had a unique look and feel. It was part of the great social experiment of the early twentieth century, when Ebenezer Howard (urban planner) designed a number of new towns in the UK. Originally intended as a Quaker settlement, the premise was that the factories would be kept separate from people's living accommodation. The town was the first in the UK and one of the forerunners of places like Welwyn Garden City and, further afield, Canberra in Australia.

One bizarre fact for you about Letchworth too, was the fact that it was home to the UK's first roundabout in 1909!

We thought we'd bought a unique property that would sell easily and then – the crash happened. Would we wait another couple of years for the market to level out, or would we just go for it knowing that anything we bought would have also lost value? We also wanted to move, because the main road outside our property had become like a race track. We thought it would be lovely for Posh and Becks to be able to move to the country and experience some freedom for the first time in their lives.

All in all, it took a year to sell our house and in the end we went for a part-exchange deal to make it happen more smoothly. A lot of house sales were falling through at the time. Jules was devastated with the delay but it was worth it in the end. We also took on far too large a mortgage, which was a mistake. Jules was the main breadwinner, so a lot of the strain fell on her. Commuting to London isn't worth the hassle and the dog eat dog world of corporate life was tough on her. We should have probably moved to a smaller house, but hindsight is a wonderful thing.

These were all first world problems, of course, compared to people losing their jobs and homes. We knew many people who were affected by the crash and it took over ten years for the country to recover. The rest is history and - as I've said – we are now living through that history.

So to move or not to move? Well, we took the plunge and looked at many, many villages and towns, but never totally falling in love with any one area or house. I used to joke with my mum that, as we had decided not to have children, we always looked at Google Earth to spot if there were large trampolines in neighbour's gardens.

So without hitting the housing jackpot, we decided to extend our search and look around the Bedford area where we had friends. Suddenly the villages started to look very promising. Many of the houses had original stone brickwork and gently rolling hills. We could even start to believe we were in our favourite holiday location, Derbyshire - where we love to camp and hike.

I would have loved to have taken Posh and Becks on another road trip to house hunt with us, but as I've said before they were terrible travelling companions. So we had to settle for just telling them about the fantastic new landscape we would be introducing them to. They looked bored (and a tad hungry), but we were getting excited.

Our new life was on the horizon.

The future looked bright, the future looked green.

CHAPTER 7

Moving to the country

It was a week before Christmas and we were stuck in traffic on the A1 near Hatfield. We had popped out to do some last minute festive shopping. When we went out just an hour and a half before there was no sign of the storm to come. The forecast had mentioned localised snow showers, but nothing worse than that. When we came out of the shopping centre clutching the Christmas goodies, it was a complete white out.

We needed to get home, as we had some last minute packing to do for our house move, the next day. What sort of fool moves a week before Christmas I hear you ask? Well, we did. We so wanted to be in our dream new home before the big day, then we could invite the whole family for a first Noel in our new surroundings. We just didn't factor in the worse winter weather in a generation.

If the trucks on the A1 were struggling that night, what hope was there for our removal van the next morning? Worse still, the weather was getting worse and those very same trucks were now failing to brake properly and skidding out of control. We were now getting seriously concerned for our safety. Suddenly just making it to Christmas Day seemed more important than moving house. Would Posh and Becks be orphaned that night?

Jules was quite scared by all of this. Her thoughts immediately turned to Posh and Becks. If mum and dad didn't make it back who would look after them? We even had an arrangement in our wills that they would be taken care of, but who would they live with. Amazing that in the middle of our present danger, our thoughts turned to our princesses - perhaps not surprising!

Somehow we made it home that night, but it took such a long time for what should have been a half hour journey. The brandy hadn't been packed yet, so our first thought was to knock back a stiff drink. It had been a scary evening and we just felt glad to be alive.

So how did we decide on a quiet Bedfordshire village called Pavenham? Our wish list was ridiculous and we'd nearly given up the search a couple of times. We enjoy exercise and sporting activities, so wanted to be near tennis courts and lovely cycling routes. We also wanted the obligatory country pub and church in the village we chose. We had seen one dream property that was just outside Bedford and overlooked fields which was idyllic, but unfortunately the price was too high. We didn't even look inside it as we couldn't stretch the budget that much. We'd looked at a neighbouring house built by the same builder, so we knew the quality was good.

We decided to book some autumn sunshine in Lanzarote to cheer ourselves up. Just as we were waiting to board the plane, a friend of ours called. He lived near the village where we had seen the dream house. He knew we had been looking at the cottage and rang to give us the news that the price had dropped drastically. Somehow we found ourselves in an easyJet queue, just about to board, putting an offer in a house we'd only seen from the outside. Only we could do this sort of thing. The house had received a lot of enquiries already in the last 24 hours so we had to move quickly.

Just as Jules was about to hand over her passport and boarding pass, the offer had been delivered. We switched our phones off as we boarded and by the time we arrived in Arrecife, we were the proud owners of a new house in Pavenham, Bedfordshire. We certainly enjoyed a few Aperols that evening.

Anyway, back to that glass of brandy after that terrifying drive. The next morning we woke early, honestly believing that the move to our new house would be touch and go. We looked out of our bedroom window and it was literally a deep white blanket of snow. The main road outside looked impassable and no traffic was moving along it, although the gritters were now out and about. Posh and Becks poked their heads one by one through the cat flap and decided that they could cross their legs for a while longer. Nature would have to take its course a bit later that morning – very wise.

I reached for my mobile with a heavy heart and called the removal company, fearing the worst. They weren't convinced it was possible, as very little gritting had taken place on the main routes. The storm had taken the Councils by surprise. We also spoke to the solicitor and they were also having trouble getting into their office. They asked us it was possible that we could sit it out for a few hours to see if it could be done? We had no choice, but with people due to move into our house too, we had no idea how all of this would pan out. Were we going to spend Christmas surrounded by packing boxes?

The hours passed and Posh and Becks decided that they would have to brave the cold. They tiptoed out, did the business and bolted back in as quickly as possible. The prospect of a long cold day and trying to move on the following Monday began to look realistic.

And then the call came. We were going to be moving! Some of the main roads were now passable and the movers would try to get to us in the next couple of hours. We were overjoyed and started to do the last minute tasks such as reading the meters and finding Posh and Beck's carry cases. They were going on a road trip.

Jules' mum and dad had spent the night with us, which was a blessing really as there is no way her dad would have fancied driving in this weather. So when the movers had got everything onto the lorry, we bundled mum, dad and two felines into a Renault Megane. The two of us in the front with two humanoids and two cats squashed into the back. Posh and Becks were stacked on top of each other on the back seat and then off we went to start our new life.

When we arrived at our new home, the movers had beaten us to it and unfortunately also rearranged our new neighbour's beautifully managed grass verges. The ice and snow had been so bad, that when they rounded the corner they had left deep tyre marks in the grass. Not the greatest way for us to introduce ourselves to the neighbourhood. (We later made it up to them and the removal company paid for the repairs).

We excitedly dashed around our new house, not completely understanding which room was which. I was walking into cupboards thinking they were rooms, for at least a week after we moved in. But the bizarre thing was that Posh and Becks got it straight away. I've never done a study about whether cats have some internal satnav system, but it certainly looked that way. They made their way round the house as if they'd lived there forever. We tried to keep them in the ensuite bathroom whilst the furniture was being unpacked. We were contemplating keeping them in for around two weeks, as per our vet's advice. They were, of course, climbing up the walls by the end of day one! We made the difficult decision to let them straight out because in their previous houses, they had settled so quickly.

Professional animal experts and vets all say you should keep your cats in for at least a couple of weeks - but Posh and Becks were having none of this. They were meowing to get out from day one. We were very worried about them especially as the house backed onto a field. We thought they'd get lost. We cautiously let them out and just stood at the door like worried parents thinking we would never see them again. The day we completed on the house we even had a local carpenter install the cat flap! As there was still snow everywhere you looked, we both wondered if they thought they'd moved to Antarctica for the rest of their lives. They'd hardly seen snow in the first six years of their lives and now mum and dad had condemned them to a Siberian wasteland. This made us think they would get even more lost and confused.

For half an hour we fretted and then one at a time they followed each other through the cat flap and straight to their food bowls. Amazing animals! All part of my theory that they are essentially superior beings or aliens.

After that and as was to be the case during our next ten years in the house, Becks grabbed the downstairs for herself whilst Posh took root upstairs. They knew exactly where they were going at all times and moved from feeding bowls to beds in no time at all.

We assigned tasks between the four of us, with Jules' mum given the job of sorting the kitchen out and making sure all the pots and pans were in the right cupboards. She did this in the freezing cold as the removal men were still coming and going. Next, Jules' niece Shauni turned up and was assigned to join Jules on the hunt for a real Christmas tree. Someone had mentioned there was a forest of them in a nearby village, so off they went.

The scene that greeted them out of the snowy blizzard was a scary man in a mask with a chain saw in his hand. It looked like a horror movie or the opening scene of National Lampoon's Christmas movie. The misty cold weather just made it look even more frightening apparently. The guy even offered to deliver the tree to our door in his pick-up truck as it was so tall. When they brought the tree home, it was far too big for the room and bent when it reached the ceiling. Once trimmed it looked amazing and luckily no squirrels had smuggled themselves in with it.

The next memory is a very special one for me and Jules (and one you will read more about later in the book). Once the tree had been decorated in all manner of baubles and very shiny often tacky ornaments, Becks plonked herself immediately under it and basically lived and slept there for six weeks. She's followed that tradition every year for around ten years. She loves Christmas!

The build up to Christmas continued at a pace and somehow we unpacked all of the boxes by Christmas Eve.

The girls' stockings were of course hung up by our lovely new wood burner, (which they'd decided was the best place to spend the whole winter in front of) and then the relatives started arriving.

Now Jules' sister has a Westie, which to be honest (and I'm no dog fan) is pretty cute. She had asked if she could bring Prince to stay for Christmas Day as he was a puppy and couldn't really be left for the day. This led to lots of worries on my part about how the girls and Prince would get on.

During the big day, Posh and Becks stayed upstairs as they are quite insular. They really only like the house when it's just me and Jules in. Meanwhile Prince stayed in the utility room and was kept happy with his turkey dinner. It was only when my sister in law's family were saying their goodbyes that the three animals noticed each other for the first time. The girls had wandered down for a feed and then took part in a bizarre Mexican standoff, by keeping as still as possible when they spotted Prince. Thus proving my theory that dogs truly are stupid and inferior to cats, he just looked straight past them as if they were statues.

Cats 1, dog 0.

After Christmas we all settled into our new life in the country and started to embrace new ways, especially the bracing winter walks right on our doorstep. One of these is a six mile return trip through farmer's fields to a country park with the obligatory pub. As spring came, we did this walk more and more. It was easy to just walk into the field behind our house and follow the tracks across beautiful yellow rape fields towards the next village.

I think Posh, (who is more inquisitive than Becks), was fascinated to see us disappearing into the field almost every day and just had to come and find out more. Each day she came a little way into the field with us before getting scared and running back home. One day, I swear she must have followed us at least a mile into the field. We were so taken with this that we wondered if we should buy her a harness as we'd seen people using on Facebook. Surely cats would hate this as they like to be free? Answer – yes! She hated it and decided that if that was the way she was going to be treated, she wouldn't ever come on our walks again. She has stuck to that ever since.

Posh does have one strange habit though. At the end of each day, she loves to walk around the perimeter of the garden, almost as if she's checking out her country estate. I think at this time of day, she feels safer as there are no dogs about. As there a lot of dog walkers on the public footpath at the bottom of our garden, both girls have to be on full alert. On one terrible occasion, a neighbour's Alsatian slipped the lead and made a beeline for Posh. As she was quite young at the time, she managed to scrabble up onto the fence and escape but she was lame for a couple of weeks later. You can imagine our reaction and a few raised voices to our neighbours! More recently, a similar thing happened and Posh was able to drag her 17 year old body onto the fence just in time. Dogs are not one of my favourite things about living in the country!

One of the funniest things that happened in the early days of moving home, was the day Posh and Becks caught a baby rabbit. It was obviously quite a novelty for them to move close to a field and we found that the amount of animals they caught for us as a gift, increased in variety and frequency. One day they brought home the poor rabbit and then the fun part started. Working as a tag team they attempted to drag the poor dead animal through the cat flap to show off to mum and dad. However, it was too big to get through and so they just brought us one of its legs. What a charming gift!

Other times they have brought in a succession of baby mice, voles and shrews for us. Some dead and some alive. The ones that are alive are always fun as we have to chase round the house madly trying to save it and returning it to the wild. The dead ones can be quite hideous because cats have a way of eating most of a rodent, but leaving a nasty looking piece of intestine. Lovely!

Jules has had the pleasure of putting on her boots on two occasions and having two very different experiences. Once when the mouse was alive in the boot (that made her jump in the air about ten feet!) and once when it was dead. The scream was just as loud both times.

No account of our time in the countryside would be complete without mentioning our wedding. We'd been living in Pavenham for four years and back together for eight, so it was now or never really. As 2012 was a leap year and as I'd already asked Jules to marry me back in 1998, it was her turn to ask me.

Jules being Jules, this was no ordinary proposal and she waited until we were on a Caribbean cruise. Now this was a large cruise ship and I did wonder if the moment would be lost among over 3,000 other people. The good news was that most people went to the early sitting for dinner, so somehow Jules managed to find a spot on the upper deck. There wasn't a soul in sight. She duly went down on one knee and the rest was a blur. We'd truly squared the circle. I was about to embark on my third marriage (two of them to Jules).

First up in the planning was to try to book the church. However, with two church weddings behind me, I wasn't sure we'd be able to pull that one off. We arranged to meet our local vicar to discuss the date. I subtly dropped into the conversation that, not only would this be my third wedding, but that the second of them had been to Jules. The elderly lady vicar slowly took off her spectacles and gave me a cold hard stare. She'd been difficult to warm to and we were struggling to keep the mood light and chatty. Her disapproval when I mentioned the two weddings. was almost too much to bear. But then she surprised us and said, "Well I retire this year and I've never come across a situation like this, so it could be a lot of fun". We picked ourselves up and smiled to each other - the first hurdle was crossed. A contribution to the church roof may have helped.

Next we planned the games we wanted on the day. Having put our friends and families through all of this before, we just wanted them to relax at our wedding. We wanted lots of fun and for it to be really casual, so we booked our local playing field and the village hall. We wanted to have a full blown rounders match and then a football game to up the energy levels even more. Jules' mum thought we were mad and said, "No one will want to mess up their lovely clothes by playing games". How wrong she was. In the weeks before the wedding, people were challenging each other on social media. The sight of people parking their gym bags and trainers under the pews in the church was certainly unique.

Both of us love the swing era of music, so we booked a "Rat Pack" entertainer. We met up with him to discuss everything. I was seriously concerned that Jules might elope with him as he was a bit of a looker. Footnote – he later went on to do quite well on Britain's Got Talent.

Everything was set for our special day.

We planned drinks for 100 people in our garden to get the festivities underway. Becks was so social and very vocal in our garden and everyone fell in love with her. By the way, if you're thinking the drinks event was a good idea, think again. It was far too much organising to do on top of the wedding. It was also impossible to get everyone moving onto the church as they were so enjoying the free drink in our garden. It took Jules' mum to open a bedroom window and bellow at everyone. She is Portuguese in ancestry and reminded me of a Lisbon fisherman's wife as she shouted out of that top window. Very scary.

All the guests then walked to the village church and it was a beautiful ceremony, singing along with the choir to some Beach Boys classics. Very "Love Actually". When I grabbed a handy tambourine and joined in on percussion, I think our stern lady vicar finally gave up on the whole occasion.

Jules' mum was talking to one of the guests, when they suddenly said, "Don't look now June, but I think I've just seen your daughter riding a zip slide and her dress is covered in grass stains". We had it all – bucking bronco, coconut shy and a shooting range.

As the evening began to wind down around 11:30pm, I remember turning to Jules and saying, "We nailed it. Can we go home to our girls now".

Posh and Becks had their mum and dad back together for ever. Well, officially at least. They have loved being country dwellers and now, nearly ten years later we have some amazing memories in this house and they've been such an important part of that. Considering that Jules and I have now known each other for 24 years, they have been one of the most consistent factors in our relationship.

This time we were back for good.

CHAPTER 8

120 over 80

The doctor's diagnosis was swift and like a punch to the gut, "I'm afraid Mr Copland that your blood pressure is extremely high. If you carry on without treatment you risk a stroke".

I was in a daze. Jules and I had always worked out. We'd done boot camp and sessions in the gym. Jules was a personal trainer, so always kept me in check. I was only 55. I was too young to die!

I called Jules on the way home. She took it badly. She just couldn't understand why I was in danger, "But you work out, you play tennis, you run! Why has this happened?"

The doctor had recommended that I use a 24-hour blood pressure monitor, to make sure that the diagnosis was correct. Perhaps I had suffered one of my "white coat syndrome" moments?

The monitor was attached and it measured my blood pressure every hour, including in my sleep. This was such a weird experience, because you never quite settle to a deep sleep. Every hour I was jolted out of my reverie by the machine clicking into life and the cuff expanding. I took the machine back to the doctors and the next morning he rang me with the results.

It was not good news. In fact it was really bad news. My blood pressure was 170 over 90 in the middle of the night – equivalent to me doing an intensive gym workout in my sleep.

At the time, Jules was working on a contract with Travis Perkins and was attending a seminar on healthy living (of all things) at their Northampton HQ. The keynote speaker was a guy called Peter who worked for a Military Fitness provider and was a close friend of ours. Jules in her capacity as Head of Communications had brought him in to the company to deliver health and wellbeing training to the Travis employees. Most of these seemed to constantly smoke as much as possible and were pretty badly out of condition. Peter gave them health tests at the beginning of their training and again every six weeks. The results were phenomenal.

Jules and I attended these sessions and their regular training in the park at Bedford. Another reason why we were so shocked at my condition.

In one of the breaks during the day at the seminar, Jules ran my blood pressure figures past Peter and his face said it all, "The results are really bad. If Martin carries on in this way, he won't make six months", he said.

I also worked for Travis Perkins as a Communications Manager. I had to drive up to Manchester that evening, deliver some comms training and stay over. Jules rang me that evening and talked me through Peter's comments. We both felt very frightened and I felt like a ticking time bomb. The fact that I was travelling around the country several times a week, delivering training was adding to my stress and condition. I began to feel for long distance lorry drivers, who do this day in day out.

By the time I'd driven home the next day, Jules had consumed a massive donut, a big cookie and a giant Easter egg. That night she'd hugged Posh and sobbed her heart out. Posh was as intuitive as ever and wouldn't leave Jules alone that night. I will never cease to be amazed at how animals do this. How do they pick up on our many moods, our arguments, our depressions and even our joy?

We talked and talked into the night. If I took the drugs, would I always use them like a prop? I would never truly know if I'd recovered because of the drugs or because I was exercising and eating the right foods. Jules was determined. We could turn this round with an even healthier diet and a better lifestyle. We agreed to give it a three month window to see if we could make a difference, otherwise the pills would be a necessity.

Now, I'm not for one moment suggesting that you should ignore doctor's advice, everyone has to make their own choice and they are the professionals. We just decided to take this course of action, but with a very definite window in place of three months to see if we could make it work. On day 90 I was going to take the drugs for sure.

Jules hit the internet again and came up with our plan of action. First, she googled all of the foods and drinks that could help lower blood pressure: the list is endless but includes celery, skimmed milk (which can reduce blood pressure by 10%), a small handful of nuts, a single piece of high cocoa solid chocolate a day, blueberries, porridge and something I'd never heard of – edamame beans.

Next we talked to Peter and asked him if he would put together a running programme for me, to tackle my cardio. We paid him for this, of course, but with the results we got it was priceless to be honest.

Then Jules worked on my all round fitness, putting together a plan of exercise which would help with my cardio, my core and a running schedule of her own to supplement Peter's programme.

So far, so good. We had the exercise regime and the diet sorted, but something else nagged away in the back of my brain. It didn't take Jules too long to spot it. I took a work call over breakfast. I'd never been a natural in the corporate world and my tension was there for all to see.

I was stressed and my reaction to my boss's demands was like a lightning bolt to Jules. There it was – I needed to escape the working week and as soon as possible.

We were lucky, Jules had always been the breadwinner; she could earn enough for us to get by. So, that very week, I handed in my notice and started wondering if the siren call of the golf course was for me. In fact I didn't learn golf for another five years and then only when I had a successful business. We appreciate that not everyone can do this and we are very lucky. People get trapped in the corporate world all the time and it is tough. But sometimes decisions have to be made, that health is more important than the salary. We made that choice.

One month into the three month programme, Jules took my blood pressure. We took the measurement three times because we couldn't quite believe it – we even changed the batteries to Duracell. I was averaging 130 over 85.

Could the exercise and the diet really be working with such amazing results so quickly? Could it be the fact that Jules was putting every blood pressure reducing food onto my plate? Who knew, but we were happy.

Over the next two months, the blood pressure continued to lower and a celebration drink was had at 120/80.

Leaving the corporate rat race behind was probably a big part of this. Absolutely the right decision, but one part of the jigsaw was missing. Was this it? Was my life on the scrapheap? I started worrying about boredom killing me, more than high blood pressure. I had known ex colleagues work until 60 and then quite literally keel over and die. That couldn't be me.

Jules was out at work and I pondered all this, petting and stroking Posh and Becks and thinking and thinking. I shed a few tears, I'm not afraid to say. I felt lonely and missing the company of colleagues. The girl's purrs tried to soothe me.

Now, what could I do to make my retirement bearable, to even make it enjoyable? Mental illness is in the news a lot these days and friends of mine have suffered badly.

The girls purred and stretched out. 21 hours of sleep ahead of them. And then it hit me. I was missing people and I loved cats. How could I combine the two in a job that would ease my stress and make me really happy? Perhaps I could become a volunteer with a cat charity?

The germ of an idea, but not fully formed, came to me. My mind went into overdrive.

Only the last week, Jules and I had tried to get cover for Posh and Becks for a weekend break we had coming up. The girls had never been to a cattery and it was better if they could be looked after in their own home. But all the cat sitters we contacted in the area had said they were full or couldn't possibly look after our needs at such short notice.

So what to do? Accept this state of affairs, cancel the weekend, or could we do it better than them? Granted, I wasn't reinventing the wheel. I was just polishing the wheel, making it run faster and better and getting it to shine to perfection.

That evening, Jules was greeted by a mad grinning man clutching two very large glasses of gin and tonic.

"Think of your blood pressure, no drinking on a school day". She was right of course. In fact, usually Jules was always right. I sometimes think if I'd stayed married to my first wife Clare, I would have been about 20 stone, spending my days reading newspapers and eating all day. Not a bad life, but not one that would get me to old bones. But this time, the gin and tonic would be needed because we had a long night ahead. A long night of planning!

I ushered her into the kitchen. It's where we eat, drink, laugh and talk, often long into the night. It's where we feel happiest. Jules and I are both quite insecure which surprises some of our friends and is the reason we found each other I think. But when we are in that kitchen, I sometimes think we could take on the world. Sometimes I wish we could just transport it with us like Doctor Who's Tardis.

Jules has a thousand ideas every day, usually by the time she has woken up. The kitchen is where I slowly take them apart and explain that, "moving to Europe is not a good idea pre Brexit, learning Portuguese is a great idea, but maybe not this week and a camper van would be lovely but not whilst the mortgage is crippling us".

I should caveat the thousand ideas criticism with the reality that, every now and again, she plays a blinder. Usually, a brilliant idea that changes our lives for the better. One of them was saying yes to me back in my export adviser days.

But this time it was yours truly, who played that blinder.

"What do we love more than anything?"

"Our families?"

"Yes, but what do we love almost as much as them, but we happen to live with them?"

"Posh and Becks?"

"Bang on".

"Great, but that's no reason to celebrate with a G&T on a school day, Martin!"

I then explained the great idea, the master plan. The semi-retirement route to happiness. The whisker-lined, yellow brick road.

"Basically I'm feline groovy" (like the 60s song"), I explained. She ignored my lame pun and I undertook to save that one as a possible name for the business. I nearly used it for this book title too.

I explained that we loved cats, we loved businesses that gave us amazing customer service and we loved dealing with people. Bring it all together and what have you got?

A five star cat sitting service, equivalent to a stay at the Ritz in London. Even now, I'm still proud of my quickest response time to a customer on email – nine minutes! They had a quote and were signed up and in my diary a day later. Suck on that – Tax Office!! Sorry, I'm still bitter about waiting on their call lines, for what feels like years of my life!

Jules, as usual, took my plan and made a spread sheet of it. That's the way she rolls. She's the organiser, the brains of the operation, the clever one.

She turned my half-baked thoughts into a workable business model. She thought of the design, the logo, the website, the competition, and how to beat them. We looked at their websites that evening and became more and more confident. The amateur websites, the poorly taken pictures of couples which made them look like they would steal Fido, rather than look after him.

We had another gin and tonic. We were supersonic. (I've listened to too many Oasis lyrics, I know).

It was a couple of months until the business truly got going. We had to choose a name for it, build a website and then we had to decide which regions we covered. The research took a long time in itself. I lost count of the numbers of pet sitters I called. Some good ones and some truly terrible ones. The good ones had a head start on us, but we would catch up with them very quickly by using our unique USP – *us!*

I wanted to use a pun, so HomeFurYou got the nod. The idea of home being in the title was essential. Not only were we looking after their furry friends, we were also making sure their home was secure when they were away.

We also decided that we would look after other small animals, but drew the line at dogs. All that walking and picking up poos, no thank you!

Next we needed to create the logo, the leaflets and the website. We pulled in favours from our friends in the corporate world, to help with the design and printing of all this. It was good to think that all this time in the business world had led to something useful, for a change. The logo had to feature Posh and Becks we decided. I'd always thought that they looked the opposite of each other in colouring. Posh is mainly white with black markings and Becks is mainly black with white features. A Japanese picture of yin and yan came to mind and we gave our designer this remit. He brilliantly captured Posh and Becks for the logo and we still use it to this day.

We had the website, we had the Facebook page, we had the posters and delivered them on many cold winter days. We had Posh and Becks on the logo for kitten's sake!

We waited for our first call.

And we waited.

Then we waited some more.

Nothing happened, not one call, not even close.

Maybe I'd got this wrong. We were offering far more of a service for a reasonable price – we'd done that research. We had our secret weapons – customer service, a response time in literally minutes - seven days a week, a shiny new website. We even had professionally taken pictures of us desperately trying to get Posh and Becks to pose. Tough gig that one as you will know, cats will not do anything they don't want to do. Posh only would play ball, Becks was out of there!

What we didn't have was a presence. Either virtual or on the street. No one knew us apart from our friends and neighbours. They didn't have cats. Damn!

Weeks went by and I even contemplated that golf course.....

CHAPTER 9

Good Morning Britain

I was sitting on the sofa one day, cursing all the money we'd spent on the business, when the phone went.

A customer!?

No, not a customer. It was the Daily Mail.

The Daily Mail!

Now, I'm not going to bore you with my politics here. You didn't pick up this book to read my wishy washy liberal views about everything. You picked it up because you like cats, I assume? However, picking up a call from the Daily Mail, was to me pretty much like having Donald Trump speed dial me. I wasn't happy. I didn't like the cut of their jib. I am, though, very polite and thought I'd let them explain why they'd rung.

The writer (who was a lovely woman called Polly) gabbled something about our story. As you know, Jules and I had been on a bit of a rollercoaster ride to get to this point in our lives. We had fully squared the circle, divorced and then a couple of years later remarried. Fairly unique you would think, but apparently not. It seemed that some famous couples were also following the same path recently. The one that Polly mentioned in particular was Phil Collins, who had recently announced he was marrying his ex-wife.

Strangely enough, we thought we were in a minority in getting back together, but it seems like an awful lot of people do this. Jules knew people in this situation when she was working at Shell, for instance. I guess it's all just a question of timing. Some people are destined to be together, but for whatever reason, the stars just aren't aligned for them first time round.

One funny incident happened to Jules at Shell, which made me laugh a lot in relation to all of this. A younger colleague of hers was going through a tough time in his relationship and asked several people in a meeting what he should do. Jules piped up with some advice from her experience and he shot straight back with, "And why should I listen to someone who is marrying their old man for the second time?" He had a point really.

Anyway, back to Phil Collins. My memories of him go a long way back. I remember being pretty much obsessed with his "divorce" album called "Face Value" and specifically a song called "In the air tonight". A song which became famous later on for a gorilla playing the drums in a chocolate advert. Anyway, my memory of it was less surreal. He played it on Top of the Pops. For younger readers, "TOTP" as we called it, was a popular music programme of "yesteryear" when groups used to come on and mime badly to their latest release. It was essential viewing every Thursday night on BBC1.

I was working at the BBC around the time of "Face Value". A few of us working there would often get free tickets to go along and watch TOTP being recorded. I remember fondly going into the BBC bar after the show and bumping into Frankie Goes to Hollywood or Culture Club. Exciting days for a management accounts assistant, who'd applied to the BBC for some glamour. When I first got the job there, I expected to bump into Adam Ant at the water cooler every day, but it didn't quite pan out like that. The accounts department was stuck out in the back of beyond, or White City, as we refer to it now. All the exciting stuff used to go on at TV Centre.

Anyway, a few of us had got tickets for Top of the Pops and on came Collins with a tin of paint on his piano. Apparently, this was a reference to the fact that his wife had left him for their decorator! His public show of hurt was somewhat compromised in my mind by the fact that he later divorced a subsequent wife by fax.

Feeling that Polly probably didn't want me to talk her through my eighties pop references, I decided to listen to what she had in mind. Apparently they had done some research and our names had come up through a PR company that Jules worked with. They would love to interview us and take pictures for a feature about remarrying your ex that they were planning. Polly said we didn't need to make up our minds there and then, so we could sleep on it.

So, we retired to the kitchen and talked it over. I laid my liberal values on the table and explained that there was no way I would take the "gutter money" on offer for being interviewed. It was only one step better than working for the devil himself. Or Rupert Murdoch, as I prefer to call him.

Jules reasoned that our story could be very romantic to lots of other couples in a similar situation and could also lead to recognition of our new business. Any publicity is good publicity in other words. Sometimes, I admire her straight talking and reasoning, but there was no way that I was going to give in on this one.

The next morning I called Polly to set up the interview – Jules won that one then.

Before the interview with Polly, we had to pose for some pictures at home to go with the article. A photographer and a make-up artist came to see us and spent about an hour setting up the shots.

We'd noticed in similar articles in the Mail, that when they photographed a couple, they always had the woman in a red dress; the same red dress! It seemed like they just wheeled it out every time they had a lifestyle article. Sure enough, the photographer carefully unpacked THE red dress. It didn't really fit Jules that well, so he pinned it at the back until it looked like it was made for her. The make-up artist then got to work and transformed Jules into a glamour model from the 1950's. Not her look at all. In fact I could barely recognise her when she came in. Her hair was sculpted within an inch of its life too. I thought that they had brought in a body double for her to be honest.

Jules is not the sort for fancy dresses and make up. She'd far rather be hanging around in a pair of shorts playing sport or keeping fit. The photo session was a lot of fun to be honest, and we enjoyed posing. We even sneaked a couple of images of us for the cat business, holding (or trying to hold) Posh and Becks.

Polly was delightful, never prying, very polite. And I have to give it to her – every word was exactly as we'd said it and nothing was made up at all. Polly told us that she was also going to interview another two couples who had been through the same thing, so we thought we might be lucky to get a paragraph or two in the finished article.

The article took a little while to be published, but when it did we dashed to our local Waitrose (no comment needed). We were greeted by the guy whose job it was to put the newspapers out. He immediately stopped what he was doing on seeing us, "Oh my goodness, it's our two celebrities". He then proceeded to call over a couple of colleagues and explained the situation to them. He was holding the Mail open on a double spread of a story and we dimly took it in that it was our article. Unbelievably, they had led with our story and printed a massive colour picture of us. The other two couples barely merited a mention and their pictures were really small.

With red faces, we thanked our new found fans (after signing autographs!) and escaped out of the store, clutching six copies of the Daily Mail. Six more than I'd ever bought in my life.

When we got the copies home, we read every word and were pretty excited, to be honest. It read really well and my wife looked like the glamour model that she always was to me. That article has "followed" us ever since and when Jules starts a new job, her colleagues always mention it. Damn Google!

Our families loved it and our friends mocked us lightheartedly and we thought no more about it until…

…we got another call.

ITV!

They'd heard from an old friend of mine who worked in the BBC about the Daily Mail article. They wanted to interview us!

"Great, I said when is the show going out?"

"Tomorrow!"

"What?"

"We need you in the studio at 7am for make-up and then you'll be interviewed by Holly and Phil at 9:30 on Good Morning Britain"

The end of that sentence disappeared in a haze. I'm sure after the word Holly there had been some other detail. But nothing else seemed to matter. HOLLY!

Now I'm a man and essentially I'm quite shallow. Strange that, I know – man, shallow. Holly is every red blooded male's idea of perfection and not since my formative years, lusting after Debbie Harry, had I felt this way about an icon. Apart from Jules, of course!

"Would we be happy to go on there for a live interview with Phil and Holly!?"

You bet!

I'm a coffee addict and needed a shot of caffeine to wake me up a bit, so I bought one at the station to drink on the train. Bad mistake – I spilt it all over me. So when we got to St. Pancras, I had to rush into a branch of Fatface to buy a new shirt really quickly!

We loved the whole experience and conquered our nerves in the green room and were again plastered in more make up. The presenters and crew were lovely and we got to stand ten yards away from the great Rick Wakeman (one of our heroes), just before we went on. David Bowie had just died and he was playing a tribute.

This time Jules wore her own dress and looked amazing. I was far too nervous when the light turned red, so Jules took over and did most of the talking. The interview was a blur but we seemed to get through it and then the social media buzz started up again, both good and bad. Lots of people wrote in and totally trashed us. I'd never been on the receiving end of this kind of blitz before, so I mistakenly tried to answer all of the comments one by one. Some people thought Jules was like a man in drag, others thought I was "punching above my weight", on and on it went. I learnt to laugh at the comments in the end. "Keyboard Warriors" are obviously quite sad, lonely people and if that's the way they get through the day, who am I to criticise them?

So after our 15 minutes of fame we were more than happy to return to the shadows and concentrate our efforts on running the best cat business there is. But it was a lot of fun whilst it lasted.

We may have made fools of ourselves, we may have been trolled on social media, but people now knew about us. Didn't someone once say there's no such thing as bad publicity?

The calls started to gradually trickle in.

Quite a few started with, "I saw you on TV (or in the newspaper) recently. I need someone to feed my cat…." The fact that they had seen us on live TV and we'd come across as trustworthy people who loved each other, seemed to matter more than any number of marketing leaflets or google rankings.

Suddenly we had ten customers, then 30 and so on, and so on. They'd all seen us on TV and had bought into this cat loving couple. Money couldn't have bought us this sort of advertising, but a free prime time slot on television certainly could.

When our first Christmas came round we were doing double figures in terms of feeds every day. Every feed was different and every cat was a delight. I truly had the best job in the world. We made friends with lots of our customers and mourned with them when their cats died. Why had I spent my life getting stressed in an office when I could have the joy of cuddling a feline and driving around without a care in the world?

When Jules is asked by colleagues at work what her husband does. She says, "He cuddles cats for a living". That's it really. I am so lucky to do this job and I never take it for granted. It has provided my motivation, my social life, some good earnings and peace of mind. What's not to like?

Plus, I got to kiss Holly!

I didn't wash for a week.

CHAPTER 10

#Bestjobintheworld

When Jules gets asked at work, what her hubbie does for a living, most people think she's taking the "mickey". But when she explains the concept behind the business they begin to say things like, "Wow, that's so cool" or "Really, why didn't I think of that?"

It really is the best job in the world, no contest. Having said that, there are risks and dangers. You are totally responsible for the health of someone's beloved animal, (basically a member of their family). Every time you open someone's front door, the cat could run out and never be seen again. That's my responsibility, no one else's. My reputation would be trashed; my business finished and the owner would probably sue me on top of everything else!

So it does carry risks. Things like losing a customer's keys are always in my mind and if I was to accidently do any damage in their properties or drop anything, I'd be liable. Luckily we have safeguards that cover us for all of this and all of the relevant insurance in place. At HomeFurYou, we take care of people's home and precious pets as if they were our own.

Talking of keys, locks, doors and alarm systems. Sometimes, inevitably things go wrong. On a number of occasions, Jules and me haven't been able to get into a house. Sometimes because the key has broken off in the door or the lock jams. We're always prepared, and carry an industrial sized tin of WD40 with us. We've had to call out locksmiths for customers who are away for at least a week, or for a shorter time sprinkled dry food through the letterbox. Our cats never go hungry.

And then there are the alarm systems. These can range from complicated set-ups to much simpler systems with a four digit code. But when they're faulty - nothing (but nothing) will stop the high pitched alarm going off. Thankfully, customers can usually cancel the alarm remotely on their phones. So far we haven't had the police arriving at the property and thankfully this happens on a very rare basis.

Most amusingly, it seems to happen to our colleague Katie more than any of us. Quite a few times she has called us saying, "Guys I'm so sorry about this, but I can't get in to the house/through the gate/I can't get out". Katie has started to take it personally and I think is a little paranoid that we are setting her up for failure. Nothing could be further from the truth and we are more than happy to come out and help. With WD40 in hand we join her at the house and then take her for a calming cup of hot chocolate afterwards. I think she now knows it's not a deliberate policy to give her the tricky ones!

On one occasion, Jules got locked in and had to climb out of a kitchen window, with Whitby (a beautiful black cat) looking on in amusement. On another, Katie got locked in a house with a Norwegian Forest cat and we had to go round to rescue her. What we later told her was that we'd also been locked in the same house. We blame the cats for deliberately messing with the locks to prevent boredom.

So having said all of that – it's still the best job in the world. Even if you didn't like cats you'd probably see how calming and relaxing it is. No nasty boss shouting down the line and no annoying colleagues, (who you wouldn't spend a minute with outside of work). Best of all, how many of us can say that our customers literally purr when we provide a good service. Perhaps don't answer that one!

My favourite days are when I have lots of feeds, usually at Easter, summer or at Christmas. I just get lost in the variety of houses and cats I see on the round. Some cats want to play for a long time and others just totally ignore me. That's what cats do, as we all know. Jules helps me out over these busy times and we also have some amazing ladies – Katie, Tina and Abi who step in when we can't manage all of the feeds ourselves. It's probably worth pausing here to pay tribute to these lovely ladies. The business simply wouldn't run without them. We trust them and think of them as part of the HomeFurYou story as much as ourselves.

So how did these amazing people get to be part of the business?

Well, we met Katie as a customer. A dedicated Religious Education teacher by day, the rest of the time a loving mother to four cats. Freddie, Alfie, Millie and Lottie are simply adorable and we've always loved looking after them. In fact, Katie has used HomeFurYou more than any other customer – well over 200 times!

So being a fellow feline fan, Katie very quickly grew to love Posh and Becks as much as we do. In their senior years, we didn't like to leave them alone overnight when we went away. We started thinking about who we knew that could stay at our house and look after the girls. Katie came to mind immediately. Next up, we needed HomeFurYou cats looked after when we were away. Once again Katie put her hand up for that. She loves them all – long-haired, short-haired, pedigree, moggies and everything in between.

Katie is the oracle on all things cat related. We've asked her tons of questions over the years about our own and customers' cats. She has a practical no nonsense approach and always knows the right answer, whether it's to do with medication, diet or just about anything else you could ever want to know in the moggie kingdom. A true star!

It's now time to introduce Tina. We know Tina through her daughter who we met at our boot camps. Charlotte has now joined the army so all that hard work paid off. Tina still lives locally and has two rescue cats. If Katie is the Cat Oracle, then Tina is known as the "Cat Whisperer". Sometimes, Jules and I almost despair of tempting a particularly timid feline from behind the sofa. Tina meets that very same cat and by day two they are putty in her hands. Does she use sleight of hand with a craftily hidden pocket of treats? Or is she employing the darker arts to win them over?

To be honest, we think she just employs her silky tones to break down their resistance. A real professional and a rock for HomeFurYou. The customers just love her.

Last but definitely not least, Abi is usually a dog person and runs a canine walking business very successfully. To be honest though, she loves all animals and her appreciation of cats has grown helping out HomeFurYou over the last four years.

Abi is an animal behaviour and welfare graduate and owns two rescue dogs, a cat and a tortoise. She brought the dogs home from the charity she supports and visits each year - Saving Pound Dogs Cyprus. www.spdc.org.uk. This amazing charity rescues dogs from the streets and the killing pounds of Cyprus. Abi has a heart of gold.

We got to know Abi because our businesses became Facebook friends and she recommended us to a customer. Now she works for us whenever she can and also even sleeps over and looks after our own girls. She just simply lives, sleeps and loves animals.

As for Jules, she just loves helping because she says it's so different from her corporate life. At work, she has to make some tough decisions and sometimes this involves reorganising teams and letting people go. So she likes nothing more than to meet some of our customers and give them a cuddle or have some playtime.

One of my favourite examples of this was when Jules had to look after a lovely ginger tom in Bedford. James, Finn's dad was pretty convinced that he loved company so much and would get lonely without him. So, he asked if we could look after his feline for a whole hour each time. (for an extra fee of course). This very "lonely" cat took one look at Jules in disgust and then promptly left through the back door cat flap. He wasn't seen again for the whole hour, so she felt a total fraud sitting in someone else's house for an hour.

One of the reasons for this type of cat behaviour is of course because they're aliens. Bear with me. This is a theory I have been building up for a number of years now.

Cats are simply waiting to take over the world and they may be a form of alien that has spent thousands of years just waiting for their moment to strike.

The way they seem so superior and only do things on their terms; they humour the stupid humanoid by playing with a fake mouse on the end of a string, or purr to pretend they love our affection. Everyone knows that their project is nearly complete and world domination lies just around the corner. Dogs on the other hand are just stupid!

With these thoughts in mind, it got me thinking, do cats simply wait until we're out for the evening, or away for the weekend to plan all night parties with the other cats in the neighbourhood, who they seem to hate most of the time. I remember Eddie Izzard, the comedian, once doing a whole routine on the thought that cats are secretly drilling for oil behind the sofa when you're out!

Is the truth that this super race of cats is really united and ready to pounce, but first let's party when the stupid parents are away? Think Home Alone, think Toy Story but with cats and lots more attitude.

So, when a cat like Finn does something like leaving Jules on her own for an hour, they know exactly what they're doing. They are unsettling us, waiting for the moment when they pounce and take control of the world. It's a theory I've been working on.

Other cats we meet have been waiting so long for the call to come, that they start attacking us or jumping to scare us. I have several examples of cats like this on my rounds. One of them literally lies down in the middle of the hallway, hisses at me and strikes out with her claws if I dare to pass. All I see is a blur of teeth and claws flying at me across the room. Another one regularly hides behind a bed and if I look over the bed to see if it's alright, it takes off vertically and attaches itself to my head. When Jules fed this cat it slashed at her arm and she started to bleed – all over the lovely white carpet the owner had just bought. We should get danger money for these two cats!

So be afraid, be very afraid, they are waiting and watching. When customers go away on holiday and we look after their darlings, be sure they are plotting when you leave the home.

Recently Jules and I had to abandon a camping trip a day early. This was due to the damp miserable weather and a bad post Glastonbury cold on Jules's behalf. I started to imagine Posh and Becks posting look-outs and saying, "OMG they are home early, stop toasting mice on the bbq; stop rolling cat nip joints; put the vodka away; start sniffing each other and whining". Could they get the word back to HQ in time to do the clean-up, or would we finally discover the truth that our house was merely a cover for the grand feline takeover?

On our return, both Posh and Becks had managed the big clear up to perfection and all of their new pals in the neighbourhood got out in time or had they just been sleeping for 21 hours while we were away? Only time will tell which of these theories is true.

I have to say though, that the majority of our customer's purrfect cats are really well behaved. But some are a little boisterous. One of the funniest incidents that happened to me, was when two of my favourite cats Molly and Jasper went full "rock star" in their house. I swear that if they'd been able to lift the TV, they would have thrown it out of the window. Now, these two were real characters and despite being very pretty cats, I lost count of the times I went round to their house and found a blood bath. Sometimes they ritually disembowelled a pigeon and other times a small rabbit was the victim. The head count became so large that I started calling them the Kray Twins!

One Christmas I remember leaving them a goody bag high up on a kitchen cupboard, out of their reach. It had lots of treats in it including an industrial supply of cat nip. Bad mistake with the Kray Twins; they got into the gift bag, ate all the treats, threw up and then basically gave the whole kitchen a dusting of cat nip. They were so out of it by the time I arrived the next morning, that they could barely wake up for their breakfast. That was quite some clean-up operation. Molly and Jasper seemed really happy with their morning's work though, so all was good. I now leave all gifts behind closed cupboard doors, for obvious reasons.

Another time, a gorgeous black kitty called Harry Potter had to be fostered with one of my customers. Everyone thought that he would be fine with two other cats, a tortoise, two hedgehogs and a jar full of stick insects. Just how wrong can you be about this kind of decision!?

Harry Potter went ever so slightly mad with all these new distractions. He's a pretty "out there" cat anyway, his favourite pastime being to walk across door frames and pose with his red neckerchief, while terrorising the humanoids below.

He had no idea what to make of the tortoise, which had just lazily woken from its winter of hibernation. He must have mistaken it for a large moving rock. So, that kept him occupied for an afternoon. Then after another day of hanging out on door frames, his attention turned to the strange collection of sticks in a jar on the mantlepiece. Harry broke the jar and the poor owner spent all week trying to find the stick insects, one of which had lost a leg.

The hedgehogs just freaked him out as you can imagine, and more than held their own, so he spent that afternoon trying to jump on the kitchen clock and removing the second hand.

However, it isn't just the feeds when I have a lot of fun, sometimes the initial meetings with the customers can be hilarious, too. One customer I met in Bedford had two very young toddlers, obviously too young to be at nursery.

So, we just cracked on with the meeting with the kids playing happily in a corner. As the meeting progressed though they got more and more interested in the two of us and especially me as I guess I was a novelty to them. I swear they had mistaken me for a human climbing frame, because as I droned on about testimonials and police checks, they had decided to jump on me and try to climb up onto my shoulder and then my head. I gamely struggled on - waffling about our pricing structure and terms and conditions, by which time they were sitting on my head.

To be fair to the mum she did ask if I wanted them removed, but I said, "Oh no, they are little darlings, it's not a problem at all". A statement I came to regret as they grabbed my glasses and decided to throw them across the room. I did get out safely in the end, with the key and a signed agreement, but I'm not sure who was laughing more, the customer or me! The customer, Enfys has again become a big friend of ours and runs an independent travel company. She sourced the trip to Nepal for us which is where we came in at the start of the book.

I couldn't close this chapter without telling the tale of how I nearly missed my wife's 50th birthday party. Jules has never been one for a big blow out for a party, but did feel she should celebrate her big 5-0 with the family and friends who are closest to her. We decided to do this at home and got in some great caterers and topped up the wine and beer supplies. So far, so good.

At the time, we were looking after some adorable ginger cats for a lady in Bedford. They were indoor moggies, but each time I went over there I was supposed to let them out for ten minutes in the garden and then feed them. That should be easy I thought, as cats are so easy to train and keep in-line. Yes, I think you spotted the irony there. Each day at around 5pm I'd gone over to the house and successfully got both cats in. Not in ten minutes mind you, more like 30 or 40.

So, fearing the worst on this Saturday early evening – the day of Jules's birthday party, I decided to leave early and get this feed out of the way. I needed to be home to help with the preparations.

I let both cats out whilst I sorted out their food and litters (I could write a whole chapter on litters by the way, but will leave it to your imaginations!). Then for the hard part; I'd let them out of the back door thinking I had got well over two hours until the party started - nothing could go wrong. When it got to over an hour with both cats still out and me crawling on my hands and knees round the back of the shed, I knew it wasn't going as planned. Then suddenly I did manage to get hold of Tracey, the friendlier of the two. I rushed back into the house and successfully locked the door. Now, I just needed Sharon. So, I literally ran down the garden, not noticing that the decking was rotten and full of holes.

My foot sank into one of these holes, wrenching my ankle and I came down with a sickening thud onto concrete. My glasses had flown off so I had no idea where they were, and I could swear my kneecap was broken in about 30 places. I couldn't move.

At that moment Jules called me and asked me where I was and why was I avoiding helping with the party? I tried to mouth my defence but the pain was so intense, that I just blurted out some random sequence of words that included knee, broken and hospital. Jules is always very practical in these situations, usually thinking that I'm swinging the lead and so just said, "Martin, pick yourself up and get back here!"

In the end everything was fine. The knee wasn't shattered, and the ankle wasn't broken. I was able to stand up eventually and limp my way back to the house. I thought I'd bring the cat in but as I made my sorry way back through the rear door, Sharon - with those mocking alien tendencies that all cats possess - flew past me and straight to her food. I grimaced and locked the door.

I didn't dance much at the party, but we had a brilliant evening. I raised a glass to Sharon and Tracey at midnight and we celebrated Jules' 50th in style. I was in severe pain and it took over six months of physio to recover.

I have the best job in the world.

Nothing could stop me feeling that way!

CHAPTER 11

Breeding like rabbits

We walked to the beautiful station in Seattle, grabbed a coffee and then excitedly boarded the train to Vancouver. Jules and I had just run our second marathon in Seattle and we were basking in the glory, whilst struggling to walk. No one had told us that Seattle was built on a series of ever increasing gradients and the marathon route organisers had decided that it would be really good fun to include every single hill.

So how did a 57 year old man end up running marathons, I hear you ask?

The marathon was one of my ten bucket list items that we decided upon on a trip to Derbyshire, our favourite escape whenever we feel life getting on top of us. The trip came soon after my diagnosis for high blood pressure and from discussing what we wanted to do with the rest of our lives. We each separately wrote down our top ten activities and destinations. Not surprisingly around a third of them crossed over between us. There was nothing morbid in any of this. In fact, at my current rate I would be struggling to fit them all in before I popped my clogs! It was more a resetting of our life plans and focussing on what was important to us. So by a lovely open fire in our favourite pub - the Fox in Hathersage, we plotted out our dream bucket list. These included hiking in Nepal, touring India and seeing the Pyramids.

Anyway, I digress. The pain of the marathon apart, it was lovely to spend some time in such a wonderful city. I'd always wanted to travel to Seattle ever since November 1991. That was that date Nirvana released their seminal single "Smells like Teen Spirit" and the genre of "Grunge" was unleashed on the world's ears. I'd been waiting for something to happen like this for quite some time. I was a big punk and new wave fan at the end of the '70s and grunge was something I could finally identify with again. Long explanation I know, but Nirvana hailed from Seattle and ever since 1991, I had been longing to see what the city had to offer.

The music scene was surprisingly disappointing and everyone kept telling me what a cool place Portland was instead. It looked like that particular train had moved along the line. That said, Seattle had so much more to offer from the first Starbucks outlet to the local delicacy of macaroni cheese, which you could buy in little boxes and eat as you walked around town. I'd also been warned about the rain though, and we came prepared with all the right wet weather gear. Boy, does it rain in Seattle! I was half surprised it hadn't been twinned with Manchester. I felt like I was an extra in Blade Runner or Seven, the two rainiest films ever!

The marathon had been tough with those hills and also whole sections without the public to cheer us on. At our first marathon (2017) in New York, the crowds had always been three or four deep with people literally willing you to the finish line. I'd found that marathon so moving that I cried three times around the course. There is something about the wall of noise that hits you at various sections of the marathon. Totally different in Seattle, it was more a wall of rain. So I was thinking about all of that as we marvelled at the American countryside, as it rushed past the picture windows of the train.

Relieved to have completed the second marathon but vowing to make the next one similar to New York, we were totally relaxed (if not a little stiff) and enjoying our holiday, without a care in the world. The journey had held several unexpected delights, such as the sight of bald eagles nesting on the seashore and the amazing service we had received from the Amtrak employees. Every single one of them had greeted us and wished us a nice day and no question was too much trouble for them.

So how had reality reared its ugly head so many thousand miles from home? How did we end up looking at a picture of six baby rabbits in total shock?!

To find out the answer to that question, I need to take you right back to the beginning....

We set up the business to look after felines, but soon were asked to feed a complete menagerie of animals, from goldfish in children's bedrooms to hedgehogs in the garden and as you know - even a stick insect in a jar.

Bedford, where we live has an enormous Italian community which dates back to the Second World War, so a lot of our customers are Italian. Their families either came to the area as prisoners of war, or they were involved in the brick building industry after the war. Bedford has one of the largest clay deposits in the country. We certainly know that to our cost, as it is back-breaking every time we try to dig our garden! When we moved to the house, we dug out two skip loads of clay to improve our soil. It was so thick you could have made a pot out of it.

The Italian connection in Bedford exists to this day. In fact it has the largest concentration of Italians outside of Italy! You are never short of great coffee or panetone at Christmas. Anyway, I digress, Sal is one such customer. He is born and bred in Bedford, but his family came from the beautiful Almafi Coast, situated on the shin of Italy's boot. He was one of our originals and again like many, has become a dear friend. He's incredibly talented and makes his own bespoke furniture. His garden is like an exotic wilderness with plants I've never seen before in this country. This is one of the things we love about working at HomeFurYou. We get to meet some wonderful people and a lot of them have amazing skills or talents. Best of all - we have made lifelong friends along the way.

Sal also turned his hand to making his rabbits think they are living in a palace. The hutches (they are too grand to call them that) are on two storeys with port hole windows and a lovely run for them in the middle. Nothing like the hutches we had in our day, which were pretty much thrown together by our dads. They even have tiny rabbit furniture inside which I'm pretty sure is wasted on them as they're only driven by two things in life – carrots and sex.

To stop them having sex, if not carrots, these rabbits were under no circumstances to be left alone and so were housed in separate cages. The owner had previously put them together and the female rabbit had produced a fine litter of eight. She was only just getting over that experience when we took over the feeding of Sal's bunnies.

That morning over breakfast I said to Jules, "You just have to come and see these rabbits, they are so cute." She explained that she was busy due to her morning fitness business, but I kept nagging her until she gave in. Jules loved working on the business and had fond memories of working the whole of the previous summer when she was between contracts. Her day job is a Communications Director but her fitness company was her true love. She was planning her next session and burpies were more on her mind that bunnies. One day she'll write that book too, as she is so amazing at it.

We get very busy at different times of the year with the business, especially Christmas, summer and Easter and I couldn't have run it last summer without her, Katie, Tina and Abi.

Off we drove to Sal's house and duly fed his three cats and then the fish in the pond. Then we walked down the end of the garden to the rabbit's cages (palaces). As they were in need of a clean, Jules suggested that we get each rabbit out in turn into a central pen and clean out their hutches whilst they ran around. No danger there we thought. So out came Flopsie (we've changed the names to protect the innocent) and we cleaned his cage. He jumped back in especially as we tempted him with fresh carrots and lettuce leaves.

Then, we got Mopsie out and started to clean her cage. Unfortunately not noticing that we had left Flopsie's cage unsecured. "Martin", Jules cried out, but it was too late Flopsie was all over Mopsie and for literally seconds he mounted her. The rabbits chased each other into the hutches and I was left with the sight of Jules' body disappearing into the cage, leaving just her bum framed nicely in the port hole window. Covered in rabbit droppings, she emerged with a ghostly white face.

I'll never forget the look of terror in Jules' eyes, as she grabbed Flopsie and lifted him up, looking for signs of sperm on his tummy. She felt sheer panic and asked me there and then to research on my phone how quickly rabbits ejaculated. Eight seconds apparently. We both breathed a sigh of relief, as we felt Flopsie had only been in action for about five seconds. Maybe we had got away with it?

We quickly put the two startled rabbits back into their cages and tried not to notice the total look of frustration on Flopsie's face as we tried to get him interested in a carrot. Jules said she felt sick about the situation. I was more terrified of GCHQ (the Government's spy network) monitoring my google searches and coming across that one. How the heck would I explain that?

I have to confess here, that I've googled some weird questions in my time, but never anything that came close to that one! There's a programme on the radio where callers mention the last thing they googled. That would certainly be an interesting one to explain away. It also seemed to me that rabbits were not renowned for their dating techniques. No candlelit meal, no soft lights and music, just wham bam, thank you mam!

We decided that despite everything looking OK and hopefully no damage being done, that we should tell Sal what had happened. He was lovely about it. Insisting that probably nothing would happen and even if it did we could have first refusal on some baby rabbits. The next day Jules went to work and during a team meeting, asked if anyone knew about rabbits. She wanted reassurance that everything would be OK. Sarah, a member of the team had kept rabbits before and seemed confident that everything would be just fine.

So move the calendar forward 36 days later.

I was idly scrolling through my messages on my phone, whilst watching the occasional bald eagle nesting outside the window, when one message caught my eye.

A picture of what looked like six wet pieces of fleshy alien?! What was this all about? Then I spotted who had written to us.

One of our customers.

SAL! Oh no!

It transpired that the average gestation period of a rabbit is indeed 36 days. I turned to Jules in the rail carriage and said, "I'm delighted to tell you that you are the proud mother of six babies!"

She was stunned and didn't say anything for a few minutes. We texted Sal back and promised to do the right thing and rehome them. He was fantastic and said the whole thing had made him laugh a lot and not to worry. He knew lots of people who would take on a bunny.

Later that evening and unable to stop laughing, overlooking the stunning harbour in Vancouver, we sipped on a cool Canadian beer. In fact, we laughed until we cried long into the night. The eight seconds that Flopsie took to quench his passion could have seen off our business. Eight seconds and that's my lot. One bad review and I'm dead in the water. In this social media driven world, all small businesses live and die online. It's how I get my customers in the first place but it's also where I can get trashed and lose my reputation. Luckily we have only had five star reviews, but two bunnies could have closed us down. So here's to no trolls and lots of rabbits in the future.

We were so very lucky that Sal was so understanding and the good news is he still uses us and he's has become one of our 100 club, (100 feeds and more).

By the way, another funny thing happened with the same customer, too. As I mentioned at the top, he had three cats. They were very distinctive. A black one, a black and white one and a ginger one. Easy to remember.

We always walk round a customer's house (with their permission) to find a cat if we haven't seen it that day. Every day I fed these cats, I counted three. Then the next day another cat was whining at the back door to come in. I didn't let it in. Same thing happened on the next day and then the next. I began to feel really bad about not letting it in. It was obviously not a stray and was well looked after. Sal must have got another cat but not had time to tell me. We kept a detailed database on all of our customers. Jules is particularly OCD when it comes to records and ensuring that everything is in its place and regimented. I'm more laid back but need her attention to detail. That's hardly surprising as she was named after Julie Andrews in Mary Poppins. Everything needs to be "spit spot" Her parents loved that movie.

As Sal was in Italy I couldn't get hold of him. So I decided to let the interloper in. He even got on really well with all the other cats and so I felt bad I hadn't originally let him in. I even gave him a name – Rossi, after the famous Italian footballer who scored a hat trick at the 1982 World Cup Finals. Did I ever tell you that I can name every World Cup final team and the scores of all the matches? Jules thinks I'm a bit sad, as you can imagine.

When I did eventually get a message through to Sal I said "All good back here, your four cats are doing fine. You didn't tell me that you had got a new one, but he's lovely. I've named him Rossi, but just wondered what his real name was?"

The message coming back said, "We haven't got a new cat!"

We drove round to the property as fast as we could, imagining scenes of devastation and chaos. Would we find the sofa with rips in it, the curtains shredded to pieces, the other cats traumatised in the corner? Was the intruder a spy, a murderer or was he just after their Dreamies stash. What would greet us when we went in? He might have fought with the other cats and injured them. They could all be sitting round smoking cat nip joints. Again, we were one heartbeat away from the loss of our business.

The scene at the house was surprisingly calm. The four cats were laid out on various beds and sofas, doing what cats do. Sleeping and then sleeping some more.

This rogue moggie would not be the end of us.

Rossi was shown the door. But as he sashayed out, I caught the merest hint of the feint he had used to beat the Brazilian goalkeeper Peres back in 1982, before he shot into the corner.

I need to take another holiday; I believe Canada is nice this time of year?

1993 Bob as a kitten

1996 Bob chilling

1999 Jules and the Arsenal football team
at Sopwell House, St Albans

2003 Posh as a kitten

2003 Jules and me with our nieces, Shauni and
Dana – responsible for naming Posh and Becks

2005 Me in Cusco, Peru. Before the Maccu Picu trek

2009 Posh and Becks cuddle up

June 2013 Jules and me get wed (again!)

2015 Jules and me at Glastonbury

2016 Jules, Posh and me start up HomeFurYou

2017 Jules and me run the New York Marathon

2018 revisiting the Romney Hythe and Dymchurch Railway

2018 Becks a very pretty Princess

2018 Becks in her favourite place

2020 Posh with those human eyes

2022 Flo, the Munchkin has a seat at the breakfast table

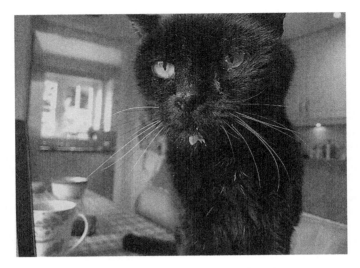

2022 Flo post breakfast covered in milk

CHAPTER 12

Becks the miracle cat

I need to say here and now, that I don't follow any conventional religion, nor do I really think there is a god or higher power. I completely accept that people do believe and that it gives them a great deal of comfort in their lives. I'm even a little jealous of that sometimes. It must be so powerful to believe in a greater guiding power, when everything in the world seems to be going wrong.

I can't explain 9/11 and I can't explain the wars that are always raging around the world. I'm at a complete loss to explain the Covid-19 virus, which is causing so much misery in families around the world right now. If the virus is proving one thing, it's that we do come together in a crisis and we do recognise the real heroes in society – the NHS workers, the care workers, the bin men, the postmen, supermarkets, the delivery drivers, the warehouse workers and everyone else keeping the country running.

So as I say, I don't believe in that big power.

But I do believe in miracles.

One happened around four years ago and it happened in the heart of my loving family.

It was October and we'd just returned from chasing the winter sun in Arrecife in Lanzarote. This was our favourite getaway and we'd been there for the last three years. It's the time of the year when they hold a brilliant street festival. In fact, it's fairly unique because the audience moves from stage to stage around the town, bizarrely following an Elvis impersonator and a brass band. You watch a band do their stuff and then the whole crowd moves en masse and onto the next one. Such fun!

We always hire bikes and spend a couple of days just cycling from town to town. All very relaxing and it gets us in a good mood to hunker down for the British winter on our return.

We arrived back home after a lovely break and were greeted by Posh and Becks who had missed us, but had been in the very capable hands of our friend Ginny (also one of our best customers). She said they'd been as good as gold and were in good health. Always music to our ears after a trip away. Ginny is godmother to our gorgeous girls and our very own Mary Poppins.

She loves them almost as much as her own cats. She started as one of our most regular customers, became a friend and even did sleepovers with Posh and Becks. We couldn't think of anyone better. Weirdest of all though – she's named in our wills! If anything happens to both of us, there's enough money to keep Posh and Becks in luxury for the rest of their days. They also get to move in with Mary Poppins. Now that is true friendship! She's leaving the area soon and shed a tear that she wouldn't be seeing them. Our girls tend to get to people like that.

Next day it happened.

Every Sunday morning, Jules and I treat ourselves to a little lie in and usually Posh joins us for a cuddle. We had long got used to the fact that she totally demanded our attention at these times. Any thoughts of a nice cuddle with my wife would go out of the window as she plonked herself right in the middle of us. I went off to get the tea and by the time I came back they would be spooning on the bed and ignoring me! I knew my place in the pecking order and I think I was basically number three on Jules's list. I accepted this with good grace; I was a very happy number three!

As for Becks, she's always been a private cat. I'm never quite sure if Posh decided the upstairs of our house was hers and Becks thought her domain was the downstairs, but they pretty much kept to this arrangement over the years. So you can imagine our surprise, when on this particular morning, Becks decided to poke her head round our bedroom door.

She started to cough and hiccup a lot and seemed quite distressed. The last time I'd known this behaviour, was when Bob came into my room all those years ago. I was immediately concerned.

We thought we'd see how she was during the rest of the day and hoped it was just a temporary bug or something. But in the back of mind, I know that cats will always come to their owners if they are not feeling very well, and so I was nervous. We basically spoilt her the rest of the day and she seemed to be sleeping well, so we thought we'd see how she was on the Monday. We weren't worried at all because she was still eating and hadn't gone to ground.

Next day, she seemed no better, so we tried to get an emergency appointment with our local vets. Our vets were completely booked up that day, so we had to ring around to get an appointment with a different surgery. I knew Becks wasn't well on the way because she normally whines until we get to the vets. This time she just carried on sleeping.

The vet we saw was quite matter of fact and even a little offhand. He seemed to imply that as she was getting older and seemed quite unwell, perhaps we should consider our options. Well we were certainly not in that frame of mind at all. We made it clear that we wanted to explore everything that we could possibly do for her. We would of course never let her suffer if the prognosis had seemed irreversible. He took some x-rays and kept her in for more tests.

That afternoon, Jules and I had a serious conversation about our feelings for the first vet. We decided that we'd ask for a second opinion from our own vets. At the end of the day, we'd always been really pleased with our vets. This time we got an appointment and we were told it was going to be someone called Andy.

As usual, we settled Becks into the car, turned on the radio and talked to her the whole journey. She, in turn, whined and hyperventilated for the whole journey, as she always did.

It transpired that Andy had only been qualified for one year. He came out and said, "Becks Copland". Jules made an immediate note to change the names of Posh and Becks with the vets, as she'd never taken my name. From then on they were called Posh and Becks Minter-Copland! She asked me at what point did we agree the girls would be called Copland? I said Minter-Copland was too posh a name for moggies!

The person before us who saw Andy came out and said, "There's a guy in there wearing his Dad's coat and pretending to be a vet!" Not exactly the words we wanted to hear when the health of our blessed Becks was at stake. Andy was impossibly youthful looking, yet when he started talking, he was passionate and so incredibly knowledgeable. We immediately felt at ease. He took Becks off for her x-rays and we waited nervously in reception. When he brought her back in again she seemed to be sleeping and quite drowsy. We took Becks home and she lapped up dinner as she always did after a car trip.

Two days later, Andy called. He advised us that there were black spots on the lungs (possible tumours) and although he said cancer couldn't be ruled out, he couldn't be sure unless she went under the knife. However, given her age, he did suggest we consider this option very seriously as she was an old lady. Now, we would do anything for her, but an operation was not something to take lightly. We didn't want her to be at any more risk than she needed to.

We didn't want to do this with a 13 year old cat. The only piece of hope we had was that it wasn't confirmed. The spots could have been benign, but there was no way of knowing without further investigation. He put her on some antibiotics and some metacam to ease the pain and suggested we see how she fared over the next week.

For one week, Jules and I went around in a daze, not knowing what to do. Should we let her live out the rest of her life and then ease her suffering at the right time, risk an operation or explore alternatives to prolong her life?

Was poor Becks' number up? No way – we wouldn't just stand around and let that happen. We both decided we'd do whatever it took to get her well. Jules always springs into action in these situations. That night she contacted vets in the US and asked for guidance. We'd heard that vets in America were more advanced in this field and so decided to do some research. The ones we contacted were very responsive and we found a vet who specialised in alternative remedies. He recommended a drug called Corpet, which is based on a Himalayan root fungi. Ironic that it was from this region, as that's where we came in at the beginning of this book.

Now, we wouldn't say for one moment that you shouldn't listen to your vet. It's always good to work in partnership with them to explore all the options, both scientific and holistic. So, we researched the data on Corpet and forwarded it to Andy. He read the documents page by page and said there was no harm in giving it a go. We even had an evening conference call with him to discuss all of this. He was the most approachable person we could have asked for, our very own "Super Vet".

We ordered the drugs from the US and, alongside this, we set about giving her an even healthier diet. Jumbo prawns, fresh liver, organic chicken and 5% fat mince. We felt guilty that Becks ate better food than some humanoids. You can always count on Jules to do what's required – just like the time I had high blood pressure. Andy also recommended the steam from a hot shower, so Becks regularly joined us in the bathroom! I'll never forget lifting her up to steam when Jules was showering and Becks' wide staring eyes seeming to know that we were trying to heal her in this bizarre ritual.

Andy also recommended rain water instead of fresh drinking water and we tried this with great success. To this day, we ask our in-laws for the contents of their water butt every couple of weeks and they both drink it instead of tap water - the cats not the in-laws. We do a sort of Pepsi challenge and put both drinks out in bowls - it's always the rain water that gets drunk. I'm not sure what magical properties might be in rain water but they seem to enjoy it. I'd really recommend trying this on your cats if they don't seem to be drinking enough.

We took it in turns to sleep downstairs with Becks, so that we could comfort her if she was distressed or ill in the night. There was nothing we wouldn't have done for her.

There is no way in our hearts that either of us was ready to let Becks go, but I think we both feared the worst when confronted with the medical evidence.

And then the miracle happened.

Day by day, she seemed to be showing signs of improvement. Soon after this, we took Becks back to Andy, who confirmed to our delight that the tumours were reducing in size. We literally hugged him! He obviously reminded us that we weren't "out of the woods" as the cancer could come back, but his grin said it all. He was basically saying that the tumours had nearly gone and all the signs were really positive.

Three months on with a huge amount of love, perseverance, a good diet and the alternative drugs, an x-ray confirmed that the tumours had disappeared….. completely. Andy was overjoyed and simply couldn't understand how this could have happened. He said, "The scientist in me struggles with how this worked, but obviously I'm delighted".

We will always be grateful for the miracle that happened and the extra time we were allowed with her. She was really chomping through her nine lives. Was it the Himalayan root fungi, was it the baby faced Super Vet, or was it her diet? Or was it simply the love that we showered on her day after day, night after night? Or was it a miracle?

I know which one I think it was.

CHAPTER 13

The naked girl in the bath

I did think of putting a parental lock on this chapter, but to be honest the humour is more of the "Carry On" variety, so it really shouldn't shock anyone!

Part of the reason I call my job the best job in the world, is the wonderful customers we have. We've become friends with a lot of them. We've booked holidays to Nepal with one, Enfys who runs a travel company and received IT support from another, Clive who does that kind of thing as his day job. Clive set up our whole system, so that from the moment a customer asks for some dates we're straight on it and respond with a quote in seconds.

We've even shared home cooked Indian meals with another couple. Delicious!

No two days in the job are the same. That's what makes it such fun. The cats are all different and I get to know them so well. Some will come out and stop you from getting on with your day at all. They want your attention and they want it now. There's a cat called Lucy who always sits on my shoulder and nibbles my glasses. There are others who greet you with such loud cries, that they melt your heart. Ollie and Sylvester come to mind here, but there are many others. Then there are the shy ones who you rarely see and if their food wasn't disappearing you'd swear they weren't there. From Tinkerbell hiding on a wardrobe to Frida never coming out from under the bed.

We honestly know our cats better than their human counterparts, as I usually only meet the owners once to set everything up. I remember once trying to introduce one of my customers at the station to Jules and saying to her, "This is Buffy's dad!" because I had forgotten his name. I also have long conversations with customers in shops and supermarkets, without actually remembering who they are. Yet I would recognise their cats in a heartbeat! My excuse is that Chris (I remembered his name!) was dressed in his business garb and I'd only met him once before in his jeans. If I'd met Buffy waiting patiently for a train, I'd have recognised her straightaway of course.

I know which cats will be noisy, I know which ones will be "stand offish", but as for their owners, I have no clue apart from their love of cats, which is good enough for me. A bizarre footnote to that one by the way. Jules is an experienced church organist and has agreed to play for Chris' wedding soon to Louisa. Amazing the connections you make running this business!

Near the top of the cat "hit parade" though, was a feline called Lilly. I can't really explain what it was about Lilly. She was demonstrative; she loved you and greeted you like a long lost friend. When I compared notes with Jules and the other ladies who help us out when we're away, everyone loved Lilly. She was never in the best of health and was only around eight years old but suffered a lot with various ailments. Even when she was on medication, she would crawl up onto my lap and would have been happy sleeping there all morning.

She stopped going out near the end but I remember Jules' last pictures of her in the garden. I think we all knew she was dying, but the super human (cat) effort she made to pose for these selfies, means that we treasure them as much as our own cat pictures. She was a special lady. Ruth her owner was one of our original customers and has stuck with us for over six years.

A lady of enormous taste, her house is immaculate and she could have been an interior designer. Jules and I always comment on some new piece that she has added to her beautiful Bedford house. After Lilly left us for the Rainbow Bridge, I think we assumed that Ruth would find it difficult to have another cat after Lilly. She obviously missed the wonderful company that our furry friends bring us and she suddenly announced the arrival of Missy. This beautiful young tabby has now stolen our hearts like Lilly. It would appear that Ruth really does know a thing or two about choosing the best cats.

Fortunately, we have a lot of fun when we do the job despite mourning with our customers when any of their cats pass on. In this chapter I'll try to tell one or two stories of incidents that have happened to me, which leave me red faced just thinking about them. They also leave me doubled up with laughter.

We might as well get this one out of the way. I'd just begun a new run of feeds for a customer. She told me that although they were going to be away for ten days, her daughter might pop in during that time just for one day. She wouldn't be staying over, so it was highly unlikely that I'd even see her.

It's always good to be warned of these things, as I have met gardeners, cleaners and friends who were just as surprised to see me as I was to see them. We also have one or two customers who get their dates wrong. When they open the door to me, it's always fun to see the slow realisation that they have given me the wrong dates or haven't left early when they said they would. Jules even let herself into a house once and overheard a conference call in with the owner of the house taking part. She said the cats face was a picture, as he seemed to be looking around saying, "Dad's on a conference call, what are you doing here!?" Jules backed up really slowly and closed the door behind her.

Talking of dads, Jules' dad still doesn't quite understand what I do for a living. I think he would much prefer if I was a doctor or a policemen or something he understands. He always says to me when I get back from my round, "Were your customers in when you fed their cats?" I always politely explain that we only feed the cats *because* the customers are away – he never quite gets it!

So back to the lady who was away. The first days feed had gone really well. I let myself in the back door and I fed their chatty moggie. All straight forward, one of the easier feeds as this cat let himself out, so there was no messy litter.

The next morning came round – a Friday. I let myself in again and do remember thinking as I looked for the cat, that I was sure I hadn't seen that half full bottle of red that was left in the kitchen. Also, had those unwashed dishes on the drainer been there before? I must be imagining things and I convinced myself that they had been there and I hadn't spotted them. So I was beginning to feed the cat, when I heard the most awful gushing of water from upstairs. Fearing that the boiler had sprung a leak I rushed upstairs, only to hear that the noise was coming from the bathroom. I headed straight in there.

I'm not sure whose scream was loudest, but I think I might have just edged it. The sight that burned into my retina when I ran into the bathroom was of a young woman, naked and desperately trying to cover herself with the soap suds, but failing. She screamed again, I screamed again and I reversed at great speed out of the door and down the stairs almost in one flowing movement. All the time shouting out, "I'm sorry I didn't expect anyone in and I thought the boiler had sprung a leak". For her part, she was babbling about how sorry she was and the fact that she'd decided to stay a night when she wasn't planning. She hoped I wasn't too shocked. As I made my exit out of the back door, the cat just looked at me with distain, as they do in these situations as if to say, "Well, did you think it was my bottle of red wine and half-finished meal you saw?!"

As soon as I got home I contacted the customer with my apologies. She just about stopped laughing, to say her daughter had told the same tale and was just as embarrassed. "Please don't worry," she said, "It's made my day!" From that day on, I promised myself I would try to pick up on clues around the houses I visited and try to avoid seeing any more naked women on my rounds.

Another occasion when you might say that I'd strayed into a situation, over which I had no control, was when Jules joined me on an evening of feeds. I'd told her about these two pedigree kittens that I knew she'd adore. The two owners were gay and very artistic and cultured. The townhouse was in a busy street and looked like many others in the town. I loved the mix of Andy Warhol prints on the walls coupled with the Kylie DVDs strewn around the living room. In fact with their box sets of The Crown, it looked the perfect domestic set up. Very suburban and quite restrained. Little did I know……

If we can't find someone's cat and they are "house" cats that don't roam outside, we always ask the customers permission to look around the house. Apart from that, we always leave any doors that are already shut as we found them. On this occasion though, we couldn't find one of the adorable kittens and I was getting worried, as was Jules. There have been quite a few situations where customers have left cats in rooms without a means of escape, as they are in a rush to get away for the weekend or the cat has sneaked in at the last minute.

So we decided to start looking around this house, opening doors and calling out to Pipsqueak (name changed to protect the innocent). No sign in any of the rooms downstairs, so we walked upstairs with a sense of dread. Had Pipsqueak been on his own for very long? It was a hot few days in summer so what if he was suffering. We checked the bedrooms, still no sign, so Jules opened the door to the last possible cat hiding place. The third bedroom. Probably a study we thought? I was still checking under the beds in the other rooms, when I noticed that Jules had stopped talking.

I hurried to catch up with her and as I walked in my eyes couldn't quite take in the scene that greeted me. Jules explained her thought process later. She said that when she first entered the room, she thought, "Oh brilliant, they have a fitness studio" as there seemed to be some kind of frame that had been erected in the middle of the room. Jules being a fitness instructor is always looking for new ideas. Her eyes then wandered around the rest of the room and she again thought, "Wow, what an interesting array of weights and all in different colours and what interesting shapes they're in".

By now, you may be forming your own opinion of what Jules was taking in, but to credit her with one endearing quality, Jules could sometimes be a bit straitlaced. I remember at a festival once, when she saw all the metal canisters on the floor and said, "Why are there so many cyclists at a festival", mistaking legal high capsules for tyre repair kits!

So, it was only when she started looking around this room in more detail, taking in lubricants, leather gimp masks and DVDS featuring a lot of men with Village People style moustaches, that I think it all sunk in. We had stumbled in on a "torture" chamber. I'll never forget how quickly she backed out of the room. Pretty much as fast as I had when confronted with a naked woman. As she backed out, both kittens meowed playfully at her. I'll never know where the second one had been hiding!

We never make judgements about our customer's lives, and we didn't in this case. We love them all and who wouldn't have a story to tell behind closed doors, or a skeleton in a cupboard. I think it was just that the work out Jules thought was going on in that room, was very different to the ones she puts on in a local park every Saturday morning!

I'm very proud of HomeFurYou and some of these stories will make me laugh for years to come.

Who else can say that in their working life?!

CHAPTER 14

Posh – A very special cat

I'm sure everyone reading this thinks that their pet is special and I don't doubt anyone at all for thinking this. Dogs, cats and other household pets can do some amazing things. Often things that make us think they're showing human traits or displaying human emotions.

Cats, in particular, seem to be very sensitive to the mood in a house. If there are arguments or conflicts going on, they seem to be affected by this. If there's a good feeling and lots of laughter the opposite is true, and they relax. We often credit cats with a level of empathy too, but perhaps that's just them purring or meowing at us when they want feeding? I hope I'm wrong about that, as I would like to credit them with a lot of the calm and peace that they bring to our lives. I'm sticking with that story.

We love both our girls, Posh and Becks very much. I'm hoping that has come through loud and clear in this book? Whilst we think Becks is a very special cat and we see her as our "princess", we do think Posh has some otherworldly qualities to her.

The first of these is her eyes. If you look into them, you'll swear that you see human eyes staring back at you. This can be quite disconcerting. Jules has often wondered if Posh has been reincarnated in this life as a cat, after spending her previous life as a human. Is she a human trapped in a cat's body?

There have been quite a few theories about cats with eyes like these. Cats shouldn't really have eyes that resemble a humans at all, as their pupils are meant to be more slitted and vertical. So, when you do come across a cat like Posh, it really makes you look twice. It's also what she does with her eyes as she really seems to look into your soul - when you stare at her, she stares back!

Although Posh is a regular moggie, there's a breed of cat that is meant to be more human looking than others and that's a Maine Coone. There's even one woman in Russia who claims to breed them to have eyes like this with human features. All I see when I look at pictures of these cats, is the terrible CGI of the recent Hollywood blockbuster, "Cats" - not Judie Dench's finest role, by the way. Whereas Posh looks genuinely human, as if she's just about to talk to you!

Some other human-like traits have been developed by domestic cats, which seem designed to earn them rewards or food. They can be especially cute when they want feeding and will talk to you more to get your attention. Or rubbing up against you to win you over. Posh will sometimes win me round to feed her. She'll then go and find Jules and make her feel guilty until she feeds her, too. Its only later that we realise we have both been taken in. Manipulative behaviour - just like a human!

One strange part of this is that cats only meow at humans to get attention, they never meow at other cats, so it seems they have evolved to make this part of their make-up and to get what they want. Clever animals.

It could be that instead of being an ex-human, Posh is descended from Egyptian cats. Possibly the most revered cats in feline history, these were held in high esteem for thousands of years. They killed venomous snakes and protected the kings dating back to the first dynasty of Egypt. They were often buried with their masters, along with possessions for the afterlife. So was Posh one of these special cats? Probably not, because I don't think her snake killing instinct would be that strong.

Cats even had their own goddess in ancient Egypt. She was called Mafdet. She was often portrayed as having the head of a Cheetah or a lion. Fierce and heroic she kept the Egyptian homes free from danger.

We often joke about how much we all worship our cats and give them the run of the house, but in ancient Egypt this was literally true. Their cats were even mummified in exactly the same way as their owners, to look after them in the next life.

Cats have been loved and adored across the ages and are also revered by many. On a perhaps more disturbing note, they're also often connected to the paranormal world. They certainly seem to have some supernatural skills which humans and other animals can't understand. This is probably connected to their extremely heightened senses. For instance, a cat's eyesight is superior to a humans in that they can see in extremely low light conditions.

Without wanting to get too scientific, the difference between our vision and cats is in the retina. This is a layer of tissue at the back of the eye that contains cells called photoreceptors…..

Oh no, I'm getting far too technical now! Suffice to say, they can see so much better than us in the dark. This was proved during a recent incident with Posh. We have recently had to buy her some cat steps to get up onto our bed at night. She's becoming an old lady and the arthritis is setting in. All night long she comes and goes on these, which doesn't always lead to the best night's sleep. She spends half the night popping out for snacks and the rest following the call of nature when she goes to use her litter in our bathroom. The litter is also a recent addition, as she used to go outside to do her business. As she's getting older, Posh now spends most of her time inside. Often we spend the night hearing her tap, tap tapping up the steps or shovelling her litter around very noisily. All good fun.

The point here is that she does all of this in the pitch black, because her night vision is so good. The minute me or Jules get up in the middle of the night we fall over all of these cat contraptions - we have no night vision. This was at its most spectacular a couple of weeks ago, when Jules went flying after coming back from the loo. Forgetting that Posh's steps were there, she went crashing to the floor. All I heard was a small whimpering voice which said, "Martin, help me!" Jules was lying down on her front with grazed shins but no real damage done, thankfully.

For all that, I still leave the lights on in the house for Posh and Becks when we're out.

If you think we're mad with the steps, we actually got the idea from our customers who seem to have a lot of variations on this theme. In fact talking of steps, one of our friends also has an elderly cat and has even built steps up to the top of their fence so their moggie can get to the top! These friends (both vets by the way) are as potty as us about their cats and had some time on their hands during the Covid-19 crisis. Forget the baking, forget writing the book – it's time for some cat steps.

Want to know the ultimate, though? In the Netherlands, someone has produced a picture book of steps that are found on the outside of flats. These let cats climb up and down to get to their owner's flats. There even seems to be a bizarre cat's honour, as they wait for each other to pass at junctions before ascending or descending.

It is also believed that cats can see energy fields, or even on a darker note are in touch with the spirit world. Maybe even spirits of people who've passed on to the next life. We certainly saw this with our cat Bob in our Letchworth house, when he seemed so spooked by our ghostly apparitions in the house.

Their hearing is also incredible. They can track rats and mice (and serpents in Ancient Egypt) just by the noises they make. They even have better hearing than dogs. They hear a wider range of sounds and a much higher pitch range than humans.

They can also discriminate between the origin of sounds better than we can, making this an ideal way to hear their prey.

Both of their ears can swivel independently of each other. Making the source of any noise pinpoint accurate.

The inner engineering of a cat's ear is also amazing. The tiny canals and chambers of the inner ear are full of fluid, which helps them keep perfect balance. No wonder they are so agile and graceful in movement.

One thing you should be aware of though, is the fact that cats don't necessarily recognise their names when you call them. But they do recognise their owner's voices in a reassuring way – thank goodness for that. So, all the years Jules and I thought that Posh and Becks knew when we were calling them individually, it was actually not one of their main skills!

Human hearing can be more variable it seems to me. When I awake in the night to hear Becks tormenting some poor mouse or vole, Jules sleeps straight through it. It's left to me to go downstairs and try to save the poor blighter's life. I sometimes succeed, I sometimes don't and Becks proudly leaves me with a small piece of indigestible mouse intestine to clean up. The point is I hear that sort of thing really well and yet put me in a crowded restaurant or at a gig (remember gigs? They were pre lockdown entertainments), I struggle to differentiate sounds. Jules can hear far better in those situations and yet sleeps on during a Becks massacre, or maybe it's deliberate so I have to clear it up!?

One of the other features that cats use in conjunction with their eyesight and their hearing is their whiskers.

Cat whiskers are highly developed sensory devices, to help the cat in the dark and steer it away from predators. At the root of each of these hairs is a follicle loaded with nerves.

Cats use their whiskers to brush against objects, to gauge the exact size and location of the object even in the dark. This proves especially useful when cats try to squeeze through tight spaces, as their whiskers are exactly the same width as their bodies.

Whiskers also give cats owners a good sense of the mood of their cat. If the whiskers are stretched taut across their face, they are tense and on edge and if they are drooping away from the face, they are more relaxed.

Given this, you'd think that blind cats would really struggle with sensory awareness. Not so. A lovely vet we once met told us about a blind cat that had been brought in. Apparently the owners told him that this cat was very aware of the space around it and had a kind of internal map of the rooms in his house. He never bumped into anything and the whiskers came in handy to negotiate any obstacles in his way.

So, when I look at Posh, what do I see? I see an intelligent, almost human like face staring back at me. I see her ancestors, too. In Posh and Becks, I see lions and tigers and all manner of big cats, I see intelligence, cunning and guile.

Most of all I see a lot of love shining back at me.

CHAPTER 15

Four seasons in one day

I was stranded on the ancient bridge dressed from head to toe as an elf. There was no way through and this was the fourth bridge I had tried. I had six feeds to do and no way of getting to them. We'd never let a customer down, rain or shine. But this looked like the first time we'd leave our feline friends famished. Meanwhile, somewhere in deepest Bedfordshire, Jules was trying to carry out her six feeds dressed as Mother Christmas. She was having the same problems as me.

Now, my job is a lot of fun but I don't always go out dressed as an elf. At Easter, you'll find me dressed as a rabbit right down to the ears and the fluffy tail. It really depends on the season. We love dressing up, but it's really to give our customers some laughs along the way. We have set up WhatsApp groups with all of them and share images and videos. This not only brings a smile into their lives, but also gives reassurance that their purrfect pets are in good hands and that their houses are secure. All part of the service. Even their extended families ask to be on these groups, so that they can keep in touch.

So, why on Christmas Day was I stranded on that bridge? Well, Bedfordshire countryside can be beautiful, which is one of the reasons I love my job. Its villages and towns are mostly linked together by the River Ouse, which snakes its way through a lot of these places. The river has a lot of beautiful stone bridges crossing it and these get flooded on a regular basis. Now, most of the time the flooding isn't severe, but Christmas 2019 had seen almost biblical rain. I half expected Moses to rise up and confront me in my elf outfit and part the waters. It had rained for weeks by this point and I'd never seen five of my regular bridge crossings so under water.

Using the wonders of satnav and our almost London cabbie like knowledge of the roads around us, we did manage to get round all of our feeds that crisp Christmas morning. But it did involve some almighty diversions and a lot of extra fuel to achieve this. We've still kept our record of never having let down a customer. When you're dealing with live animals, this is a basic, of course, in our line of work.

When we did get to the customers houses, the moggies were fairly nonplussed with our cosplay, but did enjoy the extra treats and catnip we had brought them to celebrate the season.

I guess weather like this in Britain is an occupational hazard. We literally have four seasons in one day, sometimes. We have rain, snow, lots of wind (four terrible storms at the beginning of 2020 for instance) and we now have heat waves! This book isn't the place for me to debate the realities of climate change; there are far more knowledgeable people than me in Sir David and Greta. But, unless you occupy the White House right now, it's really hard to deny that something is happening and it doesn't look good for our future survival.

All that said, the cats and pets that we look after are not really concerned with the bigger picture. They just want to be fed and watered and it's those stupid humanoids fault for messing up the planet.

So when a couple of years ago the "Beast from the East" hit the UK, we knew we had a problem feeding our massed ranks of moggies. This was a storm to rank with the worst ever seen in the country. I remember for example the hurricane of 1987, when I was living in London. Whole streets were blocked by falling trees after the events of the night of 15 October. The Beast from the East was in some ways far worse, because it threw into the mix freezing conditions and blizzard-like snow. It also lasted for nine days, not just one night.

Late February to early March was marked in the UK by extreme weather not seen in a generation. This was also one of our busier periods, moving out of the half term holidays towards the spring holiday season (a lot of our customers don't have children, so often book with us outside of the school holidays). How we managed those feeds in these conditions I'll never quite understand. Some roads were impassable, our cars had to be thawed out every day and I remember we even put the snow socks on the car.

Obviously if we were the Swedish or Russian branch of HomeFurYou, none of this would be a problem. They're geared up for this kind of thing. But here we are never quite ready for extreme weather of any kind. I remember commuting back in the eighties, when British Rail would regularly apologise for late and poor service, by saying it was the fault of the wrong type of snow or leaves on the track!

The good thing about this period was that we saw an awful lot more cats in their houses. Cats are extremely intelligent beings as we've explored earlier in the book. If they're met with extremely cold weather when they go out to follow nature's call, they do not hang around long outside. They do the business and then they are straight back in to the warmth of the central heating. House cats with litters have it even better. They look with distain at their humanoids who are struggling to get their cars started, or wear all of their clothes in the wardrobe just to leave the house. Why haven't they developed a lovely fur coat, they seem to be saying.

I remember our darling Becks during the Beast from the East trying to find a spot on the six inch drifts in our garden. I've never heard her whine so much as I did then as she tried to behave with her customary grace and ignored the litter we had kindly provided for her in the utility room. She had such dignity then and even during her illness. She was also determined to find somewhere outside. She yelped as she lowered her rear end into the snow and desperately tried to cover it up with her freezing cold paws. Such a trooper!

Of course the other extreme type of weather Britain has experienced over the last couple of years has been the heat waves. When I was growing up in the seventies, the number of times this happened in the summer could be counted on one hand.

1976 will always stay in my memory as if it was yesterday. The punk revolution was in full swing, but down in my little corner of rural Kent it seemed to bypass us. I loved the music and it felt angry and exciting to a country boy cut off from the metropolis. As Bruce Springsteen sang many years later, I was "Born to Run". Except I didn't run anywhere. At 15 I couldn't wait to leave school. My Dad was a Deputy Head in my first school and mum was the school secretary in my upper school. The only prospect for me and many of my peers, was to either work at the Dungeness Nuclear Power Station (quite possibly the most remote and depressing place on earth), or to become a sheep farmer, as our woolly cousins outnumbered us by 3 to 1 on Romney Marsh.

Then the heat wave of 1976 came and everything changed. I got a summer job with my best friend Tony (who lived two doors away) and we became travelling guards on the The World's Smallest Public Railway™. This is a narrow gauge railway which runs from Hythe at one end to The World's Most Depressing Place – Dungeness™. I've since taken Jules to Dungeness to show her my childhood haunts and I think she thought I had booked her a one-way ticket to hell. The power station dominates the landscape from miles around. The wind whips in from the English Channel over a barren terrain dotted with old fishing huts. I hope you're getting the picture? A famous film maker Derek Jarman used to live there. To this day you can see his hut and rub your chin meaningfully as you read one of his poems daubed over the cottage. It was a long day according to Jules.

Anyway, Tony and I loved our jobs. As we were interacting with the general public and not our immediate school chums, (who seemed parochial by comparison) we had a ball.

And we discovered – GIRLS!!

There was a holiday camp exactly at the half point of the railway line and this was a great source for spotting this new mysterious creature. We made many sightings of the female variety. They came in all shapes and sizes. Some were punks, who as I mentioned before seemed so exotic to us. It was as if they had been wafted in on the breeze from a tropical paradise. Others were beautiful, so fresh and vibrant and with a bizarre array of accents. Geordies, Scots and Yorkshire lasses. Suddenly our games of Subbuteo and marble championships seemed to matter for nothing.

The only trouble was that Tony, being far more confident and good looking than me, was always more successful in affairs of the heart. He always got the girl. He continued this trait down the years, too. He was the one who got into Grammar School, I failed the 11 Plus. He was the one who got to Cambridge, I ended up at Hatfield Polytechnic. He was the one who made his thousands working in stocks and shares. Then again I'm not jealous, because there was a girl who for some reason found me more attractive. Her name was Michelle and she chose me!

Michelle was from glamorous Tunbridge Wells (well, compared to Romney). I remember at the peak of the heat wave, I was hit by the full force of love for the first time and thought that life would always be like this. With Florida-like weather, I felt I was living on the set of Grease. We hung out when I was off duty and (when I could prise her away from her parents at the holiday camp) we went to the "pictures", ate ice cream and kissed.

A week later she went home with her family and I never heard from her again. In addition, the weather broke and as I walked along the seafront in the pouring rain, I thought that life would always be like this. It probably only took me nine or ten months to get over Michelle. A broken heart is hard to fix, and I was briefly tempted to become a Goth, but thought better of it. I would have been the only one in town.

The good news is that Tony is my lifelong friend and I've finally mended that broken heart by meeting Jules.

So yes, it was a hot summer that year.

We then experienced roughly 37 really average summers, until about 2013 when the next one came along. They are usually about as regular as England World Cup wins.

Then when I started the business, we got into a run of climate induced heat waves. We had them pretty much consistently from 2016-19. 2018 was one of the worst. Watching the England football team march to the semi-finals in Russia in the middle of another heat wave, gave me that Michelle-like giddy feeling again. It was all to end in crushing disappointment of course, but for a while I was in dreamland.

Meanwhile, running the cat business, the hot summer brought problems of its own. I was literally melting in the car every day and must admit to making more pit stops for ice creams and water on my rounds. The cats themselves were suffering, too. Most cats love the heat and laze around all day in it, sometimes forgetting that it can be dangerous to them. Like humans they can be subject to heatstroke and also they can suffer from skin cancer, particularly around their ears. So owners need to look out for this kind of thing.

We always find that house cats can suffer even more, because they're often left in airless, hot houses whilst their owners are on holiday. So we're always mindful of their needs. We've taken to giving them rubdowns with ice cubes, which they love. Some cats love to have the bath turned on for them, so they can take a long cool drink. One of our favourites, Valentin (a beautiful French character, who should have a string of onions and a stripy top on) always led us upstairs before we fed him. His eyes looked back on us as he showed us to the bathroom and then purred delightfully when the tap got turned on. Unfortunately, Valentin is no longer with us but we have fond memories of him spending at least ten minutes under the bath tap.

The welfare of our customers and their pets always comes first. Short of putting a deckchair out in the garden for them, there's not much more we could do to keep them comfortable. Although we do give Kylie a hot water bottle when we visit. Kylie is gorgeous – she was found living in a greenhouse as a stray. Then eventually wrangled her way into Chloe's Bedford flat for lifelong pampering. Chloe's brother, Craig has a British Blue, Nigel who was overbred and then abandoned on a roadside, losing his tail in an accident. Amazing people, taking on vulnerable cats and offering a lifetime home.

Now back to the weather. From the first heat wave of my life in 1976 to the numerous ones we live through today, some of my happiest moments have happened in the sun. The weather has blown me off course several times but I am now bathing in the sunlight of my dream job. I'm very grateful for that.

I predict clear skies ahead!

CHAPTER 16

Sleep well Princess

W e took our last road trip just a few short weeks ago. Me anxious and worried about the journey, as she'd been so frail. But a kind of miracle happened. A Becks kind of miracle. Becks loved every minute of it.

Her poor eyes which had been partly closed and covered in mucus, opened wide as she took in the sights and sounds of the journey. For a cat that always hated any car journey to the vets, this was amazing. Normally she whined and complained even if it was a ten minute trip.

This time she took it all in and as I pulled into the McDonalds drive in for a shot of much needed caffeine, she gazed up, with her beautiful princess eyes, at the server. As usual with Becks, they were under her spell.

"Oh bless her, is she on the way to the vets?" the server said. "Yes she has cancer; this is our last chance to try to save her". I replied. "But she looks so well." she responded.

And she did. On this morning Becks had summoned up one last blast of energy from somewhere.

She was loving the road trip, loving the countryside and the brief glimpses of mid-February sunshine.

We got to the vets. They were specialists and she'd been referred here after a two month illness which was affecting her face and her kidney.

Jules joined me at the vets in her lunch hour. She and I had been through an emotional rollercoaster. Posh and Becks has been with us for most of our relationship. We had no kids; they were pretty much our daughters!

Mark, the vet started his examination and then another amazing thing happened. Even before he had the chance to get her out of her cage, she got out and started walking around his consulting room. Becks was never a lap cat - everything was on her terms, but she literally jumped into his lap.

Now, she'd always preferred the company of men. Something about the tone of their voice I think. But I'd never seen this. Our miracle cat was giving us hope again.

By now you know her history. By now you know that we thought she could pull through again.

It all started two months before, just before Christmas. Posh and Becks were due their annual check up and vaccinations. We took them to the same vets but a different specialist, as the baby faced wonder that was Andy had moved on. Sarah, the new vet was lovely and both girls immediately took to her.

Posh was her usual laid back self and barely got out of her carrying case to greet Sarah. She gradually coaxed her out and was amazed when she looked up her age on the screen. "I can't believe she's 16! She looks about eight years old". Indeed she did. Posh has always loved life, eaten far too much and is very robust.

Becks, on the other side has always been regulation princess size. Quite slight in the frame and pretty, just a bit more vulnerable. The examination was going well, until Sarah noticed a small swelling on the side of her face. It looked a little like a puncture mark. When we looked closer we were convinced it might have been a small bite mark from a mouse. Becks did bring in a lot of mice. She was so gentle when she brought them through the cat flap, holding them softly in her mouth and plopping them down in front of us. When we showed little interest in the gift or shrieked for her to put it down, she just calmly decapitated it. That's the way she rolled. Always the hunter, even in her last few months.

So we told Sarah what we thought might have happened, but she still seemed slightly concerned and put Becks on a course of antibiotics

Not being greatly concerned we returned home with them both. As usual after such a stressful trip, they had the munchies and went straight to their food. Another good sign, because surely Becks wouldn't have wanted to eat if she was that ill?

Becks then spent the evening in her favourite place – firmly under the Christmas tree. She had done this every year of her life. It was almost as if she thought the strange humanoids, brought this weird shrub in from their garden just for her.

As usual, we bought our Christmas tree in at the end of November (I know we are sad!). The minute we bought it, Becks always took root underneath it and stayed there until the first week of January. We've never really known what the attraction is, but as with the humans, I think it cheers cats up in the middle of a cold dark winter.

Was it the smell of pine or was it the lights which attracted her? Well to be honest, with Becks, it probably was just exactly that. Simple as that really. Becks saw it as her winter home. She loved messing up the gold ribbon that Jules had artistically placed on the branches. Enjoyed knocking the sparkly baubles by gradually taking them off the tree one by one - she couldn't have been happier. When Becks got bored of doing that, she would hang out in her gingerbread house decorated with fairy lights. I did tell you we haven't got kids!

So as I said, Becks came home from the vets, played and slept under the tree and then snorted catnip in her gingerbread house. How could we possibly know that this was to be her swansong, her curtain call in our lives? She seemed so happy.

The first signs that things weren't right happened quite quickly. She started sneezing a lot more and not just from the smell of pine. Her face also seemed to be getting puffier. The antibiotics didn't seem to be doing the trick and she seemed a little down. But she was never short of dignity and still got up to visit the toilet outside. She never "went to ground" as some cats seem to do when they are unwell. She just seemed quieter, more insular.

We took her back to Sarah. She thought it would be a good idea to take a cell sample, so we agreed to that there and then. She also felt what she described as a lump on the kidney area, something that obviously concerned her. Jules and I exchanged glances, we were worried. We left Becks with Sarah so that she could take some needle samples from the mouth and kidney – she also arranged for an ultrasound. When we picked Becks up that afternoon, the poor Princess looked so sad as she had been shaved all over – we weren't expecting that.

We drove away trying to keep the mood positive for Becks. We've both always thought that they can pick up on their owner's moods. Posh and Becks always loved the radio on in the car, so we put it on. I didn't say a word to Jules and she was also lost in her thoughts. We were both so convinced that the miracle cat would again defy the experts.

We got home, Becks ate a lot, she went straight under the tree and then into the gingerbread house. Just a normal evening in our house. In our minds, it would only be a few days until we got the all clear from Sarah.

New Year came and went and we even felt comfortable enough to be away from her for a night. Safe in the knowledge that Ginny (Mary Poppins), would give them lots of snuggles – what an amazing person she is.

I was off feeding cats on my round that morning, carrying out the #bestjobintheworld when my mobile rang. It was on hands-free so I answered it. It was Sarah from the vets. When she asked if I was driving and suggested that I pull the car over to a lay-by I already knew.

The news was bad. Not only did she suspect that the damage to her face was cancer, she also informed me that the kidney scan had come up with sarcoma, an extremely rare form of cancer in that part of the body. Sarah advised us that she and her senior partners had never come across this type of tumour on the kidney. A Google search could not identify a single case anywhere in the world. Trying to lighten the mood a bit she said, "As with everything that seems to happen to Becks, nothing is ever straightforward." I appreciated what she meant by this as Becks was a very special cat and even then in my darkest moment, I truly believed she would shake this one off too and be free to live for many more years.

Without doubting Sarah for a moment, we called up a friend of ours Anna. Anna is a Super Vet and didn't hesitate to pop over with her husband Chris who is also a vet. You might remember this couple from earlier in the story. They are the ones who built cat steps to the top of their fence during lockdown. Anna carried out a thorough examination of Becks and backed up Sarah's diagnosis. Now we really did need a miracle.

We decided to send Becks to a specialist referral vet to discuss what options for treatment there might be. We had always decided that as both girls were getting on a bit, that we would never subject them to an operation. So that option was out.

So we awaited the date of the referral and we tried the third different kind of antibiotics on Becks. During this time, Becks showed such courage and amazing dignity. She was still going out to attend to nature, she was still eating, but slowly, very slowly the spark was leaving her. By this stage we were trying every single type of food. We were advised that the strongest smelling foods were more attractive to sick cats. So cans of sardines were opened and shared with me over lunch (on toast, of course). It was also recommended that cat food be slightly heated to enhance the smell. Jules even tried baby food and found a lovely lady in Sainsbury's who recommended some flavours – for the first time in her life she had to ask for the baby food counter. We googled and found that Brewer's yeast added to food was appealing – this worked for a while. We mustn't forget the liver, king size prawns (had to be

Duchy of Cornwall), organic chicken etc. One day I even tried to eat the prawns out of the fridge and Jules stopped me – Becks had already chewed on them and not wanting to waste had been placed back in the fridge.

The day of the referral came, the road trip was life affirming for me and the fact that she jumped on Mark's lap gave Jules renewed hope, too. I think we were both in denial to be honest.

It wasn't until Mark started outlining the course of action and treatment that we could take, that I think we knew. He didn't pull any punches, but he also didn't make anything sound final. We'd reached the point where we were now talking about making her remaining days comfortable. We were probably looking at weeks or a couple of months at most. He said all this in the most sensitive, kind way that we didn't really take in what was being said. The one we thought was the best course was chemotherapy.

We said we wanted a night to think about the next course of treatment, but we both knew in our hearts that we wouldn't go down the chemotherapy route.

We talked long into the night when we got home. We had our little family together for the last time, although we didn't know that, of course. We hugged them both close and we vowed to treasure the last days Becks had left on this earth, but never to let her suffer and to do the right thing for her. We would celebrate her for the months and years to come and we would feel privileged to have known her.

It didn't really pan out that way. Becks had other ideas.

Valentine's Day dawned and was a beautiful day. Jules said goodbye to Becks that morning and remembers to this day that she cuddled Becks and she responded with one of her trademark meows. These had been in short supply for the previous couple of weeks and I guess this is how we knew she wasn't herself. Becks had greeted everyone she met all the time, relatives and friends and family with this noise. She loved to talk.

It was a last goodbye that she uttered to Jules that morning and she'd summoned it up from the depths of her illness. One last hurrah from our angel. Jules was even late leaving for work, because she wanted to give Becks extra cuddles.

I said goodbye to Jules and went out cat feeding. I was feeling low but determined to enjoy every last second with Becks.

When I came home a couple of hours later, I was doing my paperwork for half an hour, when I heard a plaintive cry. I rushed to be with my darling and she was in the gingerbread house as if to say, "Bring back Christmas Daddy!"

I cradled her in my arms and slipped her quickly into her carry basket. I called ahead to the vets and luckily it was one of our neighbours who worked there who answered the call. Jane had lost her own dog Sammy at the beginning of the year and was still dealing with the bereavement. She knew Becks had been unwell and told me I must try and make the vets. Jane has been a tower of strength to us then and on other occasions. She "gets" animals like we do and even slept downstairs with Sammy for months when he was ill. She's a true friend.

Becks' last road trip was not as pleasurable as the previous one. There was one more sad cry which to this day I feel was her saying goodbye to me and then she passed away. I stopped the car in a layby near the park and just sobbed my heart out. This wasn't supposed to happen to the miracle cat.

To this day we are convinced that Becks chose Valentine's Day to leave us, because we wouldn't have any excuse for forgetting her. We'd never really celebrated this day but we certainly will in future. St Beck's day has a nice ring to it.

Even stranger was the fact that she showed such courage and energy the day before at the vets. She wasn't supposed to go the very next day. We think she chose that day and we also think she was saying, "Mum, Dad I don't want you to suffer any more". She was putting us out of our suffering, not the other way around.

Just one month after all this Covid-19 hit us with all of the lockdowns, social distancing and damage to our economy. We are pretty sure that Becks wanted to go before all that, too. Going to the vets during this period would have been really difficult. The thought that Becks would have been suffered, would have been hard to take.

Now you can think that I am projecting all manner of feelings and emotions on an animal. But you have to be an animal lover to believe the magic that they bring into your life and the pain they leave when they do move on. Grieving is a difficult process and that's just as true for an animal as a human, and I will touch on this later in the book.

It took Posh six weeks or so to really come to terms with her loss. Bizarrely, we felt that after they grew up and weren't kittens any longer that they'd basically ignored each other in later life. They rarely spoke or played with each other. It was only when we looked back at photos of them after Becks died that we noticed that they were almost always together. How had we missed this?

When we brought back Beck's body for burial, we found that for a couple of days we didn't want to say goodbye to her. We kept her in the guest room in a Christmas box (she loved Christmas as you know), surrounded by her favourite toys and baubles. We weren't ready to let her go just yet. The only problem was that Posh had sensed something was wrong and probably did during Beck's illness before.

When we think about it, we had lavished attention on Becks for a good couple of months and had uninentially not spent so much time with Posh. So, she was already feeling left out.

I'd noticed this behaviour and the fact that she'd become quite withdrawn, so I googled what to do in these situations. Experts seemed to think that the best thing to do, was to introduce the living cat to the dead sibling, so we tried this. It was such a moving experience as Posh sniffed Becks and even seemed to kiss her at one point. It seemed to do the trick and I think Posh then stopped looking around the house for Becks. That said, she's never gone into that spare room since.

We buried her on the third night. In hindsight, we buried Becks too late – we just didn't want to let her go. We toasted her with vintage port on one of the coldest nights of the year and reminisced about our darling for hours. We laughed we cried. Even the neighbourhood alley cat who we call Charley Brown gate-crashed the funeral. He always fancied Becks! I read the Rainbow Bridge poem that has given generations solace in their grief.

Due to Becks' love of Christmas we buried her underneath a fir tree, decorated with coloured lights and baubles. She also has an eternal light and beautiful flowers all around her. We arranged for a plaque to be made in Cornish stone with the following inscription:

Darling Becks
Our little miracle
See you at the Rainbow Bridge
Sleep well princess
Love Mum, Dad and Posh xxx

Life had changed for good.

CHAPTER 17

Letter from Becks

I remember clearly the moment I set eyes on Mum and Dad. My previous owner didn't want me and one day put me in a cardboard box along with my siblings and drove us to a stranger's house. I later learnt the house owner was a Cat's Protection foster Mum and that she would take care of us all.

One afternoon I was napping in the lounge when a lovely couple walked into the house. They'd kind faces and within a short time were on their hands and knees playing with all the kittens. I had a quick word with my sister and said, "Come on let's make an impression and get to the front of the queue". So before we knew it we were in front of the couple with our cutest expressions. I gave my sister a little nudge and we started rolling around the floor and making cute little kitten noises. We caught the attention of the couple and they started rubbing our bellies and even bent down to kiss our heads. My sister and I were in this together and determined to be fostered as a pair.

The couple had a quick conversation then left the house. I thought we had blown it and that they would never come back – but I wanted them to be our parents? Would anyone ever want us with such competition from all the kittens in the lounge? How could we stand out? Two weeks later there was a knock at the door and the same couple walked into the house with two carry baskets. My sister and I waited patiently. The couple bent down, introduced themselves as Martin and Jules then before we knew it we were in the car bound for our forever home.

We passed the sign for Eaton Socon, then a quick right and our home came into view. An old fashioned property, with a big conservatory and a large garden to have lots of adventures in. Dad parked on the drive and carried us into the house. He opened the carry baskets; we stretched and then set about exploring our new surroundings. We were so hungry and Dad opened up a couple of sachets and we had our first meal in our new home, rounded off nicely by a bowl of water.

It was time to explore the house and we found lots of hiding places, plenty of places for long naps in the sun, to watch the world going on outside. Then four weeks later, Dad suddenly opened the back door and gingerly we walked out into the sunshine. We'd never been allowed to do this and questioned if this was a mistake, but Mum and Dad were there to support us every step of the way.

That afternoon, two mini humanoids arrived with armfuls of toys and spent the rest of the day giving us plenty of kisses and we played until we dropped. We were also given our forever names – Posh and Becks. I was quite relieved not to be called Posh and felt very happy with my new name.

Mum wasn't always in the house, but Dad smothered us with love and gave us everything we needed. Not having a Mum (of the furry variety), Dad had to teach us how to behave and to respect each other. The reality is we had Dad (and Mum) wrapped around our little paws and there's nothing we couldn't get them to do. All we had to do was sit by our bowls, look up with big dark eyes and he would melt. Life was good and I remember those early days in Eaton Socon with such fondness. A few months later, we were put in our carry cases once again and moved to Cambourne, Cambridgeshire. Once again, Mum and Dad did everything they could to help us settle in and showered us with love and affection. Not having children, we really were their kids. Mum and Dad weren't living together but Mum often visited and helped with the cleaning – that's normal humanoid behaviour, right?

You probably think we were always on the move and I guess it does seem like that, but fast forward a few years on and we ended up in a beautiful home in Letchworth. Posh and I were thrilled that Mum and Dad were back together and with a loving embrace they scooped us up into their arms. The family was complete forever and we were now living in this beautiful home. Posh and I were overjoyed, loved our daily snuggles early in the morning and we had everything we could have possibly wanted. We were so deliriously happy and have often compared our life to the royal family living in Buckingham Palace. We had breakfast in bed, the best food (organic chicken and jumbo prawns) and our every demand was met. We now had both Mum and Dad as our loyal servants and in return we gave them unconditional love every day of our lives.

One day during a blizzard in December, we were put in our carry baskets balanced on top of each other and placed in the back of a small Renault with the grandparents. We arrived at our final home, a big house with straw on the roof in Bedfordshire. Posh and I loved that home, we had a huge garden to hunt for mice and rabbits. I loved bringing Dad little pressies and seeing the look of surprise on his face. My favourite game was bringing mice in late at night, which meant Dad had to put his dressing gown on and run around the hallway madly. We really did have an amazing time and nothing was too much trouble for our parents.

Then life started to change.....

November 2019, Mum and Dad put the Christmas tree up. This was my favourite time of the year. I loved sleeping underneath the tree and rubbing myself up against the pressies – I even found catnip in one which I tore open. I started to feel a bit under the weather and put it down to the colder temperature, perhaps I had a little cold. Then my lovely whiskers started to fall out and I found a little lump on the side of my face – I had such a beautiful face and this really bothered me. I went to the vets for my annual check-up with Mum and Dad. Sarah, my lovely new vet gave me lots of cuddles did some tests and well you know the rest.

Mum and Dad did their best not to cry in front of me, but I knew something wasn't right and I was growing very tired by the day. They tried everything, new foods, powders even heated my food up in the microwave so I could smell the beautiful aromas. I had some really nice weeks sleeping in my favourite basket with a view of the garden. Dad spent hours with me, enticing me to eat and growing excited when I finished a bowl of food. Every day they gave me hope and I really did believe that I would get better.

In February Dad took me on a long road trip to the vets. We stopped at McDonalds for a coffee and baby chino. I loved that trip, lots of things to look at out of the car window. Dad had Radio 2 on and the car was lovely and warm. We met the vet, Mark and he suggested possible treatments. There and then I decided that's not what I wanted and I knew that Mum and Dad would make the right decision by me. Returning home I knew in my heart that that would be my last road trip before doing the final one to the Rainbow Bridge.

The next morning, Mum came into my room and gave me extra cuddles and kisses. She was late for work, but still gave me what I needed. I talked to her and told her that it was time for me to go and that I loved her from the bottom of my heart. She was the best Mum in the world. Mum of course didn't know what I was saying and said, "See you later on tonight for Valentine's Day".

Dad went out to do some cat feeding and then when he returned I decided this was my opportunity. I cried out and he came running. I was in pain and wanted all the hurt to go away. Dad carefully put me in my basket and rushed me to the car. As we got to Bedford, I decided that enough was enough, I said a final love you to Dad and went into my forever sleep. As I floated above the car on my final journey, Dad was holding my body tightly as he sobbed.

I'm now at the Rainbow Bridge with Blackie, Snowy, Michelle and Bob waiting to be joined by Posh. When Mum and Dad eventually arrive, then I know we will be together forever.

Mum and Dad thank you for the most amazing life, you were the most loving and compassionate parents in the world. You did everything for me and I can't thank you enough for that. Every night I look down at my fir tree alight in the garden and look forward to when we can spend every Christmas together.

CHAPTER 18

Love and loss

I t's now a full ten weeks since Becks passed away. Jane, our lovely neighbour who had lost Sammy, said that you never get over it and that "normal" becomes the "new normal", we didn't quite know what she meant. We certainly do now.

Becks was such a part of our life together, alongside her sister Posh. The thought that one of them isn't here anymore has really shaken us up. We've had cats die before but there is something about one cat dying and the other one surviving, that makes this harder to deal with. If you have one cat and it dies, it's terrible. But when two cats have been such a fixture together in your life, you're torn between mourning for yourselves and keeping positive for the cat that's still living.

Cats can exhibit depression, just like humans. In this case due to losing a sibling, but they can feel it for all sorts of other reasons, such as moving to a different home or any other major life changes. The signs you should watch out for are loss of appetite, decreased activity levels and they may suddenly be more vocal around you.

Ever since Becks passed away, we've totally spoilt Posh and lavished all our attention on her. This had the effect of helping our own grief, but perhaps did the same for Posh.

The strangest thing is that she has now started exhibiting some of Becks traits. She now speaks to us a lot more which wasn't her thing before, but something that Becks always did. She's started to hang out in some of Beck's favourite places, such as her beds and her famous gingerbread house. She seems strangely calm suddenly and is back to doing her nightly walk around the garden, which she always did in spring and summer.

The walk has one minor deviation to its previous course; she stops at Beck's graveside and just sits there taking it all in. It's like she knows that Princess Becks is sleeping well and that mum, dad and her beautiful sister will all meet one day at the Rainbow Bridge.

In Posh's case, I think she's getting better, but it's taken a couple of months for her to settle down. I think she misses Becks and probably even feels lonely. We would never for a minute think of getting a new cat as Posh is an old lady now, so I see the best way forward is to spoil her rotten - that's exactly what we do!

I've mentioned before that we followed advice and let Posh see Becks' body before we buried her. That certainly seemed to help the process. There's also been some strange goings on such as robins appearing in our garden. These only usually appear in winter in the UK, so to see them in spring is unusual. I researched what this might mean and apparently robins visit when the spirit hasn't fully moved on. It's seen as a sign that the dead are still around for their bereaved relatives or owners in our case. This gave me a nice feeling of connection to Becks still.

I would also advise creating a place of remembrance for your pet when it passes on. As you know, we've had a stone created with some beautiful wording engraved on it. It's such a place of refuge, I find when I need to think or I'm feeling low, I simply walk down the garden with a cup of tea (or something stronger if needed) and I tell Becks about my day and my hopes and fears. Slightly mad if you think about it, but in many ways she is my counsellor, my confidante. And let's think about it – Prince Charles does this with his plants, for goodness sake!

The presence of Posh is a constant reminder of her sister, too. Just the fact she cuddles up to us at night, gives me the feeling of Becks doing the same.

Now I'm very conscious at this point that some people might be reading this and thinking, "I feel very sad for you Martin, but at the end of the day you've lost a pet and not a person". I completely get this line of thinking and do understand that losing a member of your family is far worse to some people. In response, I would say that Jules and I never had children. Posh and Becks have been in our relationship for 17 out of the 24 years that we've been together. They've been through all our ups and downs and they've provided solace and comfort to us and given us unconditional love. That is just as important to us as the love we receive from family and friends. Pets, and cats in our case, provide so much and can be such an important benefit to our mental health and wellbeing.

So given that as animal lovers we'll all mourn at some time, are there any coping measures we can follow to get us through this period? I've done a lot of research in this area and found some of the ideas invaluable. I'm only ten weeks into a period of mourning and I'm beginning to remember some of the wonderful things that Becks brought into our lives. Compared to dwelling on the more negative aspects, such as could I have helped her more through her illness, or did we prolong her suffering. I now know that I can be proud of what we tried to do for her.

In my research, I have discovered that when one is mourning (for a pet or a human) there are five key stages that we all go through. Some of these we will feel more keenly than others, but it does give a useful guide to getting through a difficult time.

The renowned Swiss psychiatrist Kubler Ross stated that there are five key stages to the grieving process and I feel these are just as relevant to animals as humans.

The stages are as follows:

1. **Denial of the death of your pet.** This is perhaps one that not everyone goes through, but in our case we definitely did. Becks was such a part of the fabric of our home, that we began to start imagining seeing her around the place. Every morning in the first couple of weeks, I came down for breakfast and went straight into the lounge expecting to see her in her bed. My mind just hadn't worked out that she was no longer with us. It felt very depressing initially to go through this every day.

2. **Anger with the loss of your pet.** I do remember feeling very angry at the disease that had finally defeated our miracle cat, especially as four years before she had fought off tumours on her lungs. The very fact that we saw her as a super cat, meant that for some

reason I felt let down that she hadn't beaten this. We kept saying to ourselves, "She's a miracle cat, she can do this, she will turn it round". But if the cancer was so ingrained in her poor, beautiful body, perhaps we were fooling ourselves. It took a while for this anger to fade, but we faced it and now know that anything we had tried to do wouldn't have been enough. We never made her suffer or put her on strong drugs that wouldn't have had any effect.

3. **Bargaining about the loss of your pet.** This is all about asking yourself, "Could I have done any more, did I make any bad decisions?" It's about looking yourself in the mirror and knowing you tried everything. We did.

4. **Depression.** Perhaps the most obvious symptom, this one. Jules and I were seriously depressed for weeks and it can still come up and surprise us on occasion. I don't want to mix up depression here with having a big cry, as that's so important and can be really carthartic.

5. **Acceptance.** This one definitely takes time. Stage 1 usually stops this happening for some time. But as I've said, even up to a couple of weeks ago I was still hoping to see Becks every morning when I go downstairs. That's no longer the case and I don't expect to go into the lounge thinking she will greet me with the best meow ever, as she did every day for 17 years. So I've reached acceptance. It's just my new norm.

I should at this point mention that there are some fantastic organisations out there that can offer counselling at times like this - you shouldn't be afraid to use them. Personally I haven't needed to because Jules and I have been there for each other. If one of us feels Beck's loss particularly badly on any given day, the other is there for them. If you're single or haven't got anyone who can be a shoulder to cry on, then if you live in the UK, why not try the Blue Cross? They offer a Pet Bereavement Service or Cats Protection League who have a scheme called "Paws to Listen". There will be many similar organisations available for you, wherever you live in the world.

Another good thing to do is to write yourself a letter as if it was from your cat. This is something I have done in this book as you've seen. It's amazing how cathartic this can be and it also reminds you of all the great times you had together. In our case, their story as rescue cats was really interesting and moving.

If your pet was your main companion in life, then this is especially important. The key is to just talk. Jules and I have talked well into the night about Becks and the love she gave us. Her little ways, the way she played like a kitten and, of course, her love of Christmas. It brings so much comfort.

This reminds me of one of our sadder moments running the business. A beautiful four-year-old called Atom, sadly passed away. I made the heart wrenching phone call to Bob and Terry (the owners) in Hungary - we were all in tears. Jules and I were faced with the awful dilemma, about what to do with poor Atom's body. It was the middle of summer and the owners lived in a relatively small flat. We simply couldn't leave him there for days - we had to think quickly. Jules took charge as she tends to in moments of crisis and we took Atom back to our house. We had to keep him cool until the owners returned from holiday.

We asked Bob and Terry what they would like to do with the body. They knew we had a garden, so they asked if we could find a nice resting place for Atom. When they arrived home, we greeted them and then left them to their privacy. We gave them a couple of glasses of single malt whisky to toast Atom. The touching scene as they carried him to his new resting place and their tears of grief were too much to bear.

They've both been back on numerous occasions since. They will always be welcome to come and spend some moments with their beautiful cat. We think that Becks is looking after this youngster to this day and showing him the ropes at the Rainbow Bridge.

If you're spiritual or religious you'll have your own ways of getting through. I personally find a lot of American poetry a tad smaltzy, yet when I read the Rainbow Bridge poem as we buried Becks, I was in floods of tears. The words just engage at such an emotional level.

Although I miss my most vocal companion (she was so chatty to everyone, including strangers) I have reached a peace inside me and Becks is no longer suffering. She's in a good place and very much missed by her sister. But she's looking down on us and that pretty, princess face is smiling with love.

Love and loss do go hand in hand, but love really conquers all our darkest fears.

Sleep well Princess x

CHAPTER 19

Love in the time of Covid-19

Jules has been a professional organist for over 30 years and used to play church services every week. Then the corporate world took over and she never had the time to keep playing, especially as her job took her abroad. So when we moved to the country ten years ago, we were adamant that she'd get the opportunity to start playing again. These days she does short term working contracts, so has more time for herself.

She now visits the church at least once a week and even plays for the odd Sunday service, wedding or funeral. This is brilliant for me, because I never saw her play years ago and I can now appreciate her talent close up. The other reason she needs me there is that in winter churches can be quite scary places to be. We've both seen apparitions in one church locally and even just walking through a graveyard at night can be a bit spooky. To me this pales into insignificance compared to the cold of a church.

Even in spring it feels like you will get frost bite and it's not uncommon to wear a woolly hat and gloves. I console myself by making scalding hot chocolate and stealing the odd penguin biscuit (sorry God) from the church supplies. Funny thing is that my mum and dad went through the same scenario years ago, as he was a church organist. My mum used to do the sitting at the back of the church freezing to death. It feels like a family tradition really.

It was on one of these practice session evenings at the end of March 2020, that Jules and I went to Stagsden church near our village. No one at this time knew of the terms "social distancing", or "stay home" or "Covid-19". What we did know was that we were to be careful when greeting other people. We could rub elbows and we must wash our hands for two minutes or so or whilst singing "Happy Birthday".

Life was becoming a bit strange, but we had no idea yet that 2020 would be one of the most memorable years in everyone's lives - not necessarily for the right reasons. That night we'd heard that Boris Johnson, the UK's Prime Minister was to make an important announcement. The rumours were that for the first time in our lives, we were to go into "lockdown". It felt weird and I don't think any of us had an idea what it would mean to our daily lives.

23 March – one of those "Kennedy" moments when we'd all remember what we were doing that evening. We'd both seen the movie 'Contagion' a week or so before and also 'I am Legend', but they were Hollywood ideas of a world without people, weren't they? That could never happen on the streets of the UK, or around the world, could it?

Given the warnings of what was to come, we'd made sure to stock up with food. Of course our darling Posh had got plenty of tuna, cat food and treats to see her through the 12 week period, that had been rumoured for lockdown. We didn't stockpile like some people did though and bizarre runs on toilet paper left us all scratching our heads.

Back in church. I was listening to Nimrod by Edward Elgar played by my amazingly talented wife. I'm not particularly religious but if I was, I'd definitely be feeling the presence of the Lord. The music surrounded me and seemed to be bouncing off the church walls. Like all great music, it connected on such an emotional level. It seemed to sum up the importance of what was just about to be announced. So at 8pm we got my mobile out and listened to Boris.

Fast forward three weeks….

It's truly frightening what has happened to our world in these last few weeks. I'm sure when Covid-19 first broke out in China, none of us thought it would affect us here. Now suddenly the whole world has shut down to varying degrees. This is early on in the lockdown and we're all struggling to cope. I think the fact that we don't have an end date for this is the truly scary thing. We've been told to stay indoors for 12 weeks, but who knows if this period will be extended. There are no restaurants, no cinemas, no bars and worst of all for me – no coffee shops!

Sometimes I think Becks must have been saying to us, that she knew what was coming. When she left us on Valentine's Day, the world was pretty much the way it had always been. Shortly after, we were self-isolating and social distancing. Vets are not open, so it would have been hard to get any treatment for her. When Posh needed her quarterly pedicure during lockdown I had to drive to the vets and call them from my car. The masked vet came out to the car park and at a socially acceptable distance, collected Posh. You just couldn't have predicted this kind of thing.

My business too has taken a hit like so many other small businesses around the country. I had a full diary full of customers all going off on holiday, but obviously now that's all changed.

There is a slightly unsettling feeling to all of this. But then again, some good already seems to be coming out of it too. After four years of arguing about Brexit and people behaving with anger and rudeness to each other in all sectors of public life, a change seems afoot. People have started to be more decent and kind to each other; there's less pollution in the sky; people are really beginning to see the NHS for the shining beacon it is; we're all learning to shop locally; keep fit more in the comfort of our own homes. Children are being taught online or sent work to do by their teachers as the schools are closed. As a result, you see wonderful family groupings out and about in the spring sunshine. No ipads, no phones – people communicating with each other.

Will we remember to live this way when everything returns to "normal"? I'm not so sure, but maybe if everyone just keeps one thing from the brave new world we are living in, then perhaps a new way of living might emerge. Maybe we'll all think a little bit more about the way we want to live going forward, but that's no bad thing.

Personally, we've made plans for life to be different. We're going to shop locally from farm shops; we've discovered more walks on our doorstep rather than going away so much. We'll give Posh even more of our time (if that's possible) and we've attempted home baking. I'm also learning guitar and we are starting Portuguese lessons. This week I had to laugh, because someone on the radio said you don't need to start lots of new hobbies; write a book during lockdown; feel guilty if you haven't learnt a new skill. We've gone the other way, which is probably quite annoying to some people! In fact, I am writing this book during lockdown, so a big tick to that one!

The truth is that this is a difficult time for both humanoids and cats. No one seems to know when this will end and they can again book holidays, go to a restaurant or, even more importantly, see their families.

As lockdown restrictions are lifted, life is slowly returning to normal (whatever "normal" means now). Some shops and garden centres have opened and even football will be back soon (behind closed doors). But the world will look very different and in some ways better as I've said, but we must never forget the sacrifices people have made to get through this. The weekly clap for carers and key workers has been inspiring and they need to be rewarded and recognised for their contribution. Posh even sits with us on the doorstep at 8pm every Thursday to join us for the NHS clap. Her clapping leaves a lot to be desired because of her soft pads, but she does try.

Jules was missing her exercise classes, so she organised online sessions every week. She set these up on a new app called Zoom. Now no one had ever heard of Zoom before, but overnight this video sharing company became one of the richest in the world and its founder a multi-billionaire.

Jules unfortunately lost her job at the beginning of the lockdown, but was lucky enough to get a new one fairly quickly. She now manages a team entirely by Microsoft Teams and even jokes with them that she'll probably never meet them and sometimes wonders if they have legs, because she only ever sees their heads and shoulders.

We started to mend things instead of throwing them away and we make coffee at home rather than going out and paying for it at inflated prices. Jules even gave up caffeine completely by going cold turkey. Now that's something I'll never contemplate in the brave new world!

Queuing has become the new norm: queuing for shops, queuing for garden centres which got so bad that we now do almost all of our shopping online. Now, of course, we're very lucky as we live in the country and some people don't have that luxury. It must have been quite a trial for people who live in flats and apartments in the middle of town. Our lockdown has been comparatively easy, but this takes nothing away from people who have had bad experiences including loneliness, mental illness, domestic violence and not forgetting the terrible death rates. The sacrifices of everyone should never be forgotten.

One of the saddest occasions for Jules during the whole period was attending her mum's 80th birthday celebrations. We were supposed to be going away with her mum and dad but of course that got cancelled, so we just turned up in their garden and had to wish her happy birthday from 2 metres away. Strange days.

Jules and I are massive music fans and one of the hardest things for us to accept was that Glastonbury was going to be cancelled. I'd even bought a Sgt Pepper outfit and a Beatles wig as Paul McCartney was going to playing. Never mind, in the new spirit of just enjoying life for what it is, we're going to hold our own "Glasto" in our garden with our tents and music stages – we're the stars of the shows. Thinking about that, I hope that when we come out of this, celebrities will be forgotten. Footballers and rock stars will mean nothing to us as our new heroes are the nurses, the carers, the supermarket workers and the postmen. At least that's what I hope will happen.

In the cat world, life will be just the same as before of course.

Just with more cuddles from the humanoids.

CHAPTER 20

Back to Base Camp

The Heathrow Customs Officer wasn't happy. My suitcase made its way along the wrong channel. That sinking feeling we all get rose to the surface. We'd got stuck in traffic and it was touch and go whether we made it through security and on to our plane to Nepal.

He beckoned me over and said, "Sir, I'd like to check your bag please as it's come up with a potentially illegal substance". He started swabbing my hand luggage. And then, there it was in his gloved hand, the mouse covered in catnip. "I'm going to have to test this sir". I groaned. I thought of trying to explain it and then my thoughts wondered off to a crushingly sad time in my life, just nine short months ago when Becks passed away.

Thankfully, Jules and I made that plane to Kathmandu from Heathrow by the skin of our teeth. The Customs Officer had finally let me off the full body search, after we protested that we weren't smuggling drugs, but the toy mouse was indeed covered in cat nip! I imagined him having a sudden attack of the munchies after sniffing it, just like Posh and Becks always used to. He let me move on with my journey with a sneer and a few choice sarcastic words.

On the plane, I gathered my thoughts. 2020 had been quite some year and sad in so many ways. Not least because of the spread of Covid-19 around the world and the terrible suffering it had brought in its wake. Even this trip had been in the balance until a few weeks before as the restrictions on flights had only just been lifted. The plane was deliberately half full and many of the passengers were wearing masks, ourselves included. If life ever returned to normal it still had a long time to go until that day. A vaccine was a good six months away and so we had to accept the changes to our daily routine.

The trip to Everest had been planned a couple of years before, as part of Jules and I putting our bucket list items together

Well, we had already run the marathon (in New York in 2017 and even a second one in Seattle a year later) so our thoughts started to turn to the next one on the list – walking in Nepal and getting to Everest Base Camp.

We'd originally planned the trip a year before, so it wasn't initially about paying tribute to Becks. Fairly early on in the planning, we were at a family gathering with my Uncle and Aunt, or Michael and Rosemary as we prefer to call them. They were keen walkers and had completed the Camino de Santiago twice before, so we got to talking about our upcoming challenge. They seemed visibly excited for us and it only seemed right to ask them if they fancied joining us. They are slightly older than us so we thought it might seem a bit too challenging. They said they were flattered and jumped at the opportunity.

Separately both couples had been training for the walk at altitude and all four of us even went to London to spend time "at altitude" in a simulation pod.

So as the four of us saw the wheels of the plane leave the ground at Heathrow, we all toasted each other as soon as the drinks trolley wheeled round. It was then that I produced the cat nip mouse that Becks had loved so much and started explaining the story. Half expecting to be ridiculed for celebrating the life of a pet, it wasn't long before Michael produced a toy bear with its own miniature passport. We knew we were amongst friends!

The rest of the flight was uneventful, but between bouts of films and sleep we were getting more and more excited. When we arrived in Kathmandu, it was late afternoon and so there was no real time to explore the city, so we just settled into our hotel and caught up on some more sleep. That evening we met our fellow trekkers over a drink. Little did they know that in 14 days time they would be celebrating the life of a cat! The guide talked us through the itinerary to come and our excitement levels were now at fever pitch.

On the next day we rose early and were all slightly nervous about the flight to Lukla. This is one of the most difficult runways a pilot can attempt. A tiny pocket of tarmac nestled in front of gigantic mountains. If the pilot failed to land it was very possible that they would just plough into the scenery. I can't honestly say how many of my fellow passengers watched this unfold, mainly because I was shielding my own eyes.

At Lukla we were already at 2,860 metres and this was part of our acclimatisation. The idea was to undertake a short series of treks to get used to the climate. Some fared better than others and (as in Machu Picchu) I was very interested to note that the fittest looking people weren't always the best at trekking at altitude. There were no rules for who coped and who didn't. Unlike Peru though, everyone managed this and in fact made it to Everest Base Camp, but we'll come onto that.

We overnighted in a lovely tea house in Phakding and then another highlight of trip was waiting for us the next morning. We made our way over a suspension bridge which was literally swaying in the air. Exhilarating! We were beginning to think this would be a trip of a lifetime.

Every step of the way, Beck's cat nip mouse was pinned to my rucksack. The guides thought this was fascinating and when I explained why I was doing it, they said that cats were not often seen in Nepal. Apparently, this is because there are so many dogs that the cats are afraid to come out very much. When I mentioned that I would be saying a prayer for Becks and holding a spiritual ceremony, they again seemed surprised because although there are official days of worship for dogs, no such days exist for cats.

From Phakding we made a steep ascent to Namche, the gateway of the Himalayas and stopped again for the night. The food we were given in each place was amazing. I've had some Nepalese dishes back home, especially near Folkestone where I grew up as there are a lot of Ghurkhas stationed there. But these meals were on a different scale, so fragrant and tasty. Most of them were vegetarian and this seemed a good choice on a Himalayan trek as none of us wanted to be ill.

From Namche, we headed for Khumjung and then Phortse over the next couple of days and the views were gradually becoming better than ever. Stunning mountain passes and glimpses of the world's highest peak, were becoming regular occurrences. Another constant theme throughout our walk, were the prayer drums we saw in each village. These took the form of a cylindrical wheel on a spindle. Spiritual prayers written in the Nepalese language of Newari were written around the wheels. These and the prayer flags we saw all around became strangely comforting to us, and a colourful backdrop to our progress.

As we continued to climb, our steps were getting slower as the altitude took hold. Luckily, the trek had been carefully planned to get us ready for this, but it was beginning to take its toll in terms of our breathing and the occasional headache.

So we were glad to get to our next destination, Dingboche. We were accompanied by several sightings of the traditional Nepalese bird, the Danphe and more mountain goats than I thought it possible to see in one place.

The reality of what we were undertaking was now concentrating my mind. We were just two stages from Everest Base camp itself and I started thinking about what Becks would have been doing this time of year. I've mentioned her love of Christmas and it was incredibly sad to be decorating the tree (her tree) just before we came out to Nepal. We're complete Christmas "nuts" in our house and always trim the tree in the third week of November and so the tradition was followed as usual.

Except this year it was different of course. Jules did her amazing job with the baubles, I added the lights and then we sobbed our hearts out, almost as much as we had done on Valentine's Day when she passed away. Becks as I've mentioned, literately took root under our Christmas trees for 16 years and this year she wasn't there. It felt wrong and we felt lost without her. We tried to encourage

Posh to take her place, but it was never her thing. To be honest, I'm not sure either of us minded switching off the tree lights as we headed to Heathrow at the end of November. Becks made our Christmas every year.

Meanwhile the trek was offering us stunning views of ice glaciers at Dughla and even a side trip to Tsho Rolpa glacial lake, before coming in to our penultimate stop before Base Camp, Lobuche.

It was on this evening that we all had our first alcohol of the trip. We hadn't wanted to make the altitude sickness any worse up to this point. We all felt we deserved one little treat for nearly reaching our destination. So we tried the local concoction, Raksi. This is a strong tasting beverage quite reminiscent of gin or vodka. A bit of an acquired taste, to be honest! It did though taste like nectar after 14 days of abstinence. I asked if I could syphon off a little of this as I thought it would be needed for the ceremony on Base Camp. So I took just enough for ten small glasses for everyone.

The next morning, after next to no sleep because of our excitement, we began the final trek to Base Camp. First we hiked to Gorak Shep and although only a short distance it was quite challenging because of the high altitude. From there we followed in the footsteps of the late, great Sir Edmund Hillary and Sherpa Tenzing Norgay who began their ground-breaking trip to reach the highest place on earth in 1953.

We began our final trek up to Everest Base Camp!

When we reached our destination, the colour and noise took me aback a little at first. Were most of these climbers really about to commence the last part of their trek to the summit? Some of them seemed too "gung ho" or ill prepared. Were the walking companies just taking their money for the sake of it, without adequate preparation or training? I'd seen far too many documentaries about the subject to know this was probably true. The bodies of unsuccessful climbers which apparently littered the route to the summit bore testimony to this fact.

However, I wasn't going to let any of the tourist like atmosphere here spoil our achievement and the real reason we had made the journey. It was possible to find some peace even in the midst of this chaos. We moved away from the crowds and I asked if my fellow trekkers and Jules, Michael and Rosemary wanted to join me. They all said yes, and even the guide seemed fascinated after our earlier conversation about cats.

The next moments were for her, my princess.

I was proud of myself for the little ceremony. I was ready for this moment as I searched through my bag for the cat nip mouse. The very mouse that Becks had been inseparable from. I placed it on a pile of rocks beneath the prayer flags that seemed to dominate the horizon at Base Camp. I chose a good position, with the peak of Everest disappearing into the blue sky. Then I whispered these words to her through the streaming tears that fell from my eyes.

"Enjoy your view, princess from the top of the world. Sleep well darling Becks..

Mum, dad and Posh will always love you".

CHAPTER 21

Going with the Flo

E verest wasn't the end of the story.

In our little corner of the world, the situation has changed for ever. We no longer have our darling Becks (she is never forgotten), but we do have another kind of miracle in her place – the "Munchkin" herself – Flo!!

Flo or Florence, to give her the full name has been with us since last spring and she is 20 this year. To find out how this came to be I need to take you back a couple of years to the day we celebrated out 100th customer for the business. This was such a milestone for me and Jules as we had strived so hard to make a success of HomeFurYou. From those unpromising beginnings when we had a handful of customers, to our lucky break in the newspapers and on TV, when the customers started to trickle in initially. Then eventually they came in their numbers as our reputation spread.

So customer 100 was a big deal.

The humanoids were called Linda and Tim and the cats were called Dylan and Flo. A brother and sister, Dylan and Flo charmed us from the start. Although quite elderly even then (17) they both had such personalities and used to run down the garden path to greet us after an afternoon chilling in the undergrowth. Dylan was predominantly grey with the widest eyes and his party trick was the silent meow. Flo was jet black with the same wide staring eyes and one half of her whiskers were white and the other side were black. She was pretty much stone deaf and Jules used to love coming up behind her as she would jump into the air as she wouldn't see it coming.

We fell in love with them and they seemed to accept us immediately. It got so bad between me and Jules that we used to fight over who would feed them each time, often we just decided to do it together to keep the peace.

Before all of this, I met Linda and Tim at the initial meeting and I remember thinking that I was really happy that my 100th customers were such nice people. Well anyone who could have produced cats as delightful as Flo and Dylan would have to be nice. We gave them a bottle of champagne and arranged a photo shoot for social media and the kitties posed nicely for the pictures. By the way, in case you're wondering their names come from an old seventies children's BBC programme which used to come on before the 6pm news called the Magic Roundabout. Classic viewing when I was growing up!

We fed Flo and Dylan several times over the next few months and I remember we were quite jealous that Linda and Tim owned a property in mainland Greece where they liked to escape from their demanding careers.

And then we heard some devastating news from them. Dylan and Flo were elderly cats and not in the best of health. Dylan had the early signs of cancer and Flo suffered from quite a few ailments such as a heart murmur and kidney problems. But it was Dylan who was becoming a concern. He was seen by a vet at the end of 2020 and they gave Linda and Tim the impossible choice that all cat lovers find so difficult. Dylan was dying and could be kept alive with drugs or even invasive surgery, or he could be allowed to die with dignity. Quite rightly they chose the latter and wanted to remember him the way he was.

Now usually in these situations we receive a call from the customer or often a WhatsApp message stating that someone's beloved pet has passed onto the Rainbow Bridge. Not this time. Straight out of the blue, I received a call from Linda who told me the news about Dylan. We were devastated of course as we had loved him as much as one of our own. We just dreaded the next time we would go round to their house and only see Flo, mourning her brother. But Linda had other ideas. She asked us if we wanted to see Dylan one last time before he went to the vets the next morning. She said that her and Tim would leave the back door off the latch and go to the lounge (Covid-19 was raging so everyone needed to be careful). We could spend as long as we wanted with Dylan and could cuddle him and say our goodbyes.

Now I remember on our way over to the house that night, that we were dreading this. Surely it would be unbearable to see Dylan so close to his last day on earth and we wondered if we could keep it together. The reality was very different. Flo and Dylan both ran up to us that evening as if it was just a regular feed. They let us play with them and cuddle them to our hearts content. It was odd being in Linda and Tim's house without seeing them but it felt like an honour and one of the most moving experiences we have had running the business. I then made the mistake of looking at Jules and we both dissolved into streams of tears for this plucky little cat. What joy he had given us in such a short time. We decided when the right time would be to leave and we whispered our teary goodbyes to him. Our hearts went out to Flo who would soon be left on her own without her playmate.

It was a sombre journey home. But as I said we felt so honoured to have been given this opportunity. What an amazing bond we have formed with our customers.

The next day Linda and Tim said that they had taken Dylan to the vet and he had gently fallen asleep in their arms. Hopefully he has now joined Becks, Bob, Blackie, Snowy and Michelle at the Rainbow Bridge and they wait there this day for us to all join them and play together.

As Flo was quite frail herself and very elderly, we half expected to hear that she would follow Dylan - thankfully she didn't. Late spring; we received a call from Linda. They had decided to finally retire. They had fallen in love with Greece and wanted to move there permanently. We were delighted for them as friends and even harboured a secret wish to visit them out there.

Our next thought - about a second later, was what of poor Flo?! She would be far too old and delicate to travel out with them. Linda was already half way through covering that one. "Did we know any of our customers who would be prepared to take her on?" It would be an enormous responsibility of course, but all food and vets bills would be covered. We think Linda was secretly hoping we'd adopt Flo and that we were the only people for the job.

They just wanted to know that she would go to a loving home, for her few remaining months. We of course said we'd ask around and certainly had a few ideas of the right people for the role. Then again we just hoped that Flo would settle as she had been with Linda and Tim for all of her life. Of course, Linda and Tim wanted to keep Flo and take her with them, but they knew she wouldn't survive the journey. So they needed the next best thing – her final home and someone who would love her like they did for the rest of her days. This was a heart-breaking decision that they didn't take lightly.

Having lost our own princess Becks, the year before we would have been prime candidates ourselves to take Flo on. But, we dismissed it in the same breath as Posh would never allow another cat under her roof, would she? Posh is a feisty lady and doesn't suffer fools gladly. We'd also read that integrating two cats (especially elderly ones) was extremely tricky.

So that would never work.

Would it?

But what if?

I have to say that we did ask round our friends, family and customers. But either they weren't ready to have another cat or they didn't think it would be a good idea with their existing animals. We were drawing a bit of a blank.

Secretly, I think we were quite pleased because we fancied taking on Flo for ourselves. She was a delight, she was full of character and she just made us laugh as she appeared to think she was a dog not a cat – following everyone round with big round puppy eyes whenever we saw her.

But there was only one HRH in our house and that was the diva that was Posh. Flo would have to fulfil a minor royal role in our household, roughly equivalent to Beatrice or Eugenie.

But it wasn't going to happen anyway.

That was when we struck on a plan. We would take Flo on a trial basis for two weeks and if Posh wasn't happy her wishes would be respected – that was important. Linda and Tim did have an offer from friends in Luton if it didn't work out, so no pressure.

So the decision was made. Flo would join us for a couple of weeks in late spring. We read every book on the subject of integrating cats and set about making it work. We figured that Posh would just put a kindly paw round Flo's shoulder and they would cuddle up each night and learn to live with each other. Before that nirvana though, we wanted to put in place the steps that had worked for other pet owners.

On the day that Linda brought Flo over, we were a bundle of nerves. We decided to settle Flo into the guest bedroom with all her paraphernalia – beds, feeding bowls, water fountains, toys and scratching posts. Nervously, she took root under the bed and it makes me laugh to think that Linda lay down beside the bed on one side and I was on the other. We proceeded to have a long conversation about everything under the sun talking under a bed! In any other situation this would appear quite weird I'm sure.

Gradually, Flo got used to the room and by the end of the afternoon, that trademark inquisitiveness was in full Flo (excuse the pun). That dog -like countenance of looking up adoringly was breaking our heart and particularly Linda's. This was after all a very tough call for Linda. Linda and Tim had set their hearts on a new life, but they knew that this meant they would have to leave their beloved Flo behind. To be trusted with her remaining months and years was such an honour for Jules and me. Fostering such a darling was a privilege.

Anyway, back to that integration. Over a period of a week, we initially kept the girls apart. They fed separately and slept alone. But bit by bit, we gradually introduced them to each other. Sharing a bit of food here, sharing the smells on bedding there. Posh pretty much lived upstairs - as she had since Becks' passing and we allowed Flo the run of the house downstairs. After a week or so, it got to the time when we introduced them to each other on each side of a door. Flo seemed fascinated by Posh and tried to nuzzle up to her. Posh was nonplussed and just walked away.

When we finally introduced them properly in the garden, Posh decided she'd had enough and just took a swipe at Flo. She wasn't impressed at all with this interloper. What had we done? We seriously considered calling the whole thing off and a life in Luton loomed for Flo.

There was just one more chance to make things right. We invited the "Oracle" Katie over. She met Flo and Posh - we waited with baited breath for her wisdom. Eventually after a lovely BBQ on a summer's evening, she laid it on the table for us. "Guys, Posh and Flo will never love each other. They are two elderly cats who have had things their own way for far too long. Give up on them cuddling at night or hanging out together. Just let them have their own safe space in the house and they will co-exist. They will be happy and contented and only when their paths cross will they have a fight".

Simple when you look at it that way isn't it? But she was bang on the money. Why hadn't we seen it?

So Flo has the whole of the downstairs to herself and Posh lives upstairs, with regular foraging trips to steal Flo's food and her regular promenade round the garden. They get as much love and attention from us as before and they know the pecking order – HRH Posh is the top royal and "minor royal" Flo knows her place.

If only it was that easy! Flo follows Jules and me around the house most of the time. Ruining breakfast and meal times by trying to eat our food. The days of romantic candlelit evenings have gone forever as Flo trails her tail in everything, so it wouldn't be safe. She's referred to as the Adventure Cat. When Flo first moved in, she tried to escape twice over the garden fence. As she's stone deaf, we were worried that she wouldn't hear one of the dogs using the public footpath adjoining our garden.

One of Flo's trademark funny moments happened Christmas 2021. As the massed ranks of the relatives arrived and I fixed gin and tonics, I became worried that I couldn't find Flo. This wasn't her style; she normally loved new people and sidled up to them like a puppy dog. She was nowhere to be seen. OMG! Had she escaped out of the front door, when everyone brought in their overnight bags? Flo normally made a bolt for the front door so it was possible. I organised a search party and everyone started looking. We tried the back garden, the front garden, all around the Close and even as far away as the High Street (quite some distance away). Jules and I were in tears, having feared this for so long with Flo's adventure ways.

At 9pm on Christmas Eve, we activated the neighbourhood search team. Jules was sliding around in the mud in her high heels. The consensus with the relatives was that "Christmas was ruined" unless we found her. And it certainly would have been.

Finally, and in despair we walked into the kitchen covered in mud. We were beside ourselves and resolved to search for the whole night. This was when we heard Jules' very deaf dad say, "I think I just heard a cat meow". We ignored him as he couldn't have possibly heard a thing and also Flo had a silent meow, so how could he have heard her. But, wait there it was again. A whiny plaintive cry and it seemed to be coming from the gin and tonic cupboard. I had left the cupboard open for a split second two hours ago when Jules had called to say they were on their way and time to fix a drink.

Flo!

She was in the house!

Christmas was saved.

As she sauntered out and demanded food as if nothing had happened, we knew that our time with this darling was going to be very precious and a lot of fun.

So with Posh and Flo co-existing, we have an entente cordial, peace in our time. A happy home and our family is complete again.

By the way, if you're thinking of integrating two cats in a similar way, it isn't a decision to be taken lightly. But if it works out, it's extremely rewarding.

So, there you go. Becks waits for us, Posh rules over us and Flo brings us so much laughter and love. Good times. And our friends in Greece stay in touch to follow Flo's progress.

And on the subject of friends.

Something really good has happened for Jules and me as we ease out of lockdown. In the "windows" between tiers and full lockdowns, we have started to cautiously start travelling again. Whether it's a masked flight to Lanzarote or a week -long lodge trip to Center Parcs. We've tried to embrace the new flexible way of taking a break.

But for every one of those trips, we need a reliable support network to look after our darlings Posh and Flo. As one is 18 and the other 19, that involves someone staying over to look after their every whim. We trust Katie, Abi and Tina to do this of course, but when not available we really do have a dilemma. This is why we started looking at a professional pet sitting company. The real benefit is that everyone they use is police vetted, with great reviews from previous customers. You have to remember that you're letting a stranger into your house - you may not even meet them before you go away! In our case we insist on seeing them the night before. We're often very nervous before this happens. What if we don't like them, what if the cats don't like them, what if they are mad axe murderers?!

Well, we've been incredibly lucky on three occasions. And two of the couples have turned into lifelong friends. I remember waiting anxiously to greet Simon and Lucie one evening. Well, we needn't have worried; we got on like a house on fire and talked all night, not going to bed till 2am, even though we had an early ferry to the Isle of Wight. Jules and I were heading off to our first festival since lockdown. An amazing sunny weekend, kicked off by a Red Arrows display and finishing with some '80s nostalgia from Duran Duran.

Si and Lou were our kind of people and that night they literally changed our life. They were vegan, so we didn't attempt to cook for them. But as we listened to their arguments for their lifestyle, we felt inspired. We've now embraced the plant life and we're enjoying a new way of living. They live in Kent and last Christmas, we met them at the amazing Dickens festival in Rochester.

Friends for life.

The other couple came through the same company and having initially been disappointed when Si and Lou were unavailable for our dates, we chose Sue and Alan. Again, a long night ensued with lots of great wine and food. They had similar interests including hiking and travel and the evening just flowed by.

Best of all they adored Posh and Flo and we used to love the wonderful pictures and videos they sent us, basically providing a HomeFurYou standard of service.

In fact the experiences were so good, that we don't dismiss one day also working for an organisation such as this. When Posh and Flo have moved to the Rainbow Bridge of course. What better way of seeing the world and getting to spend a lovely time with some great furries. Both couples pet sit all over the world, so there's really no limit.

Maybe we'll just go with the Flo and see where life takes us!

CHAPTER 22

Angels and Robins

I never wanted to write this chapter.

Never.
Ever.

I stood in the freezing car park with tears streaming down my face. One of our close friends Anna (Super Vet) was with me and had given me moral support on this fateful journey. Jules was visiting her mum and dad. Following Anna's guidance I had made the decision to call the emergency vet. I didn't want to upset Jules on her journey home so decided not to talk it all through until she was safely home.

Anna works for a company that specialises in referrals from other vets. The tough cases, the impossible cases, the second opinions and the miracle cures. Anna dealt in hope and that was what we needed right now.

Our HRH Posh had not been well since Christmas with a bad cough. I think we got through the early weeks into the New Year by convincing ourselves this was asthma and treatable. But by the time of the second consultation and x-ray, the vet gave us the awful news that there appeared to be spots on her lungs consistent with cancer.

As you know, we had been here before with Becks four years ago - we didn't intend to just accept this diagnosis. Becks had survived that original illness and Posh if anything was a stronger cat. She had never been ill, always robust and we fully expected her to reach a ripe old age. Nearly 19 was good for starters. Her pure feistiness would see her through.

Oh, her feistiness!

Posh is such a moody girl, always has been. She never suffers fools gladly and is always there with a growl or a hiss for anyone and everyone. That's what we love about her. Jules and I knew how to handle her. But for newbies you needed the user manual. Rule number one – never wave your hand in front of her. Rule number two – never approach at face level. This was quite a large manual!

I remember when our great nephew (aged three) was introduced to Posh on our bed. Jules made the mistake of being distracted and not monitoring the situation. She looked back in horror as she saw Posh coming down on the unfortunate "ankle biter" from a great height. Leaving a perfect Harry Potter like scratch on the youngsters head. He had made the schoolboy error of mistaking this cute ball of white and black fur as a new playmate. Posh wasn't up for that, no way!

Luckily when Jules took the sobbing boy downstairs it was quite dark in the room. So no one really noticed just how close to one of his eyes the new minted scar was. Well at least not until they got home and I had to fess up.

That's why we love our girl. She's fiercely independent and a nightmare if she doesn't know you. But with us, she's literally a pussy cat and as loyal as a dog. Either nestling under Jules desk when she's been working at home over the last couple of years, or snuggling up to us every night. Ever since Becks passed away, she has pretty much lived in our bedroom and been inseparable from us. When my hip pain (too much tennis since the age of four) was unbearable in the night, she even seemed to know to nestle up to me in exactly the right place each night, to alleviate the pain.

A special cat as we said earlier.

Talking of hip pain, just two short weeks before the start of this chapter I finally had that bad hip replaced. Two nights in hospital was my nightmare, not because of the pain, but because my baby was not well and I didn't want to be apart from her. Jules was amazing though – feeding her by hand and making sure she was drinking lots of water to counteract the steroids she was on. But then the bloating came. Our poor beautiful darling suddenly began swelling in her paws and on her abdomen, to the point where even walking was difficult.

Still we weren't going to give up. We booked her in at the vets again to see what could be done about the swelling and she was put on diuretics. But each journey was taking its toll. Neither Posh nor Becks had ever been great travellers. A trip to the vets was always accompanied by a cacophony of whining and hyperventilating. That's how our girls rolled. Strangely enough though, I have friends whose cats love travelling and they even take them to dinner parties and out for trips. Bizarre.

But for Posh, her spirit was waning with every new drug that we gave her. We hated putting her through all of this, but as usual in these situations you have to balance the hope with the thought that your beloved animal isn't suffering. It's a fine line. The hope that kept us pushing on, was the fact that suddenly Posh was eating so well.

All the text books tell you that when an animal is ready to move on, it will go to ground, stop eating and seemingly stop caring. Posh wasn't doing that, so we carried on.

But the bloating didn't go and her walking became terrible. She never seemed to give up though. That dignity was there for all to see, as she still made the regular trips to her litter and kept eating.

If you looked deep into those human eyes of hers though, something was missing. She looked tired, she looked sad. She stopped purring. That last one killed us. Posh had an award winning purr, the queen of purrs.

We knew this was serious.

Then that fateful Sunday came round. Before leaving for her parents, Jules said to me, "Why don't we invite Anna round to take a look at Posh. I'm not for a minute saying that this is the last chance saloon, but it would just be good to get a second opinion". I agreed "Great idea, she's bound to spot something we've all missed and we'll have her back on her feet in no time". I don't think for a moment Jules or I was kidding the other one. We both knew a big decision was coming.

So Anna knocked on the door and our life was about to change forever. I first introduced her to the newest member of the household, Flo. I explained that she was nearly 20 years old and was still suffering from arthritis, kidney problems and a heart murmur. Flo just sauntered up to Anna, like she was a puppy or a kitten not an ageing moggie. She loves new people. We call her the Munchkin. (from the Wizard of Oz). It just seems to suit her.

And then with my hip almost deliberately slowing me down, we began the walk up the stairs to see the queen. Now Posh knew Anna already. We'd once asked her over to clip her nails - we were far too tense to do this ourselves. True to form, Posh took a lovely chunk out of Anna's arm and from then on, they were best of friends. This time the lady was more frail and not in the mood for a scrap. I think Anna was shocked by her bloated appearance and began taking her pulse and feeling for any obvious obstructions or problem areas. She took her time but when she was ready to speak she said, "I think we need to get her to an emergency vet. Her breathing is heavy and difficult and there is a slight heart murmur I'm picking up."

Her diagnosis was that she feared that the build-up of fluids, could have been caused by a heart condition. This was making fluids gather around her vital organs. I remember hearing all of this but not really taking it in. The next few hours were also a blur, but it was beginning to hit home. And all I could think of was Jules saying, "Don't contact me until I get home because I can't deal with bad news". Knowing that if I didn't contact her, she would know it was bad news anyway.

Anna suggested I make a trip to the emergency vets which I sorted pretty quickly. We arrived within half an hour. Anna had a bit of a dilemma as she was from a referral vets that this vet used regularly. She said she would remain in the car whilst I met the vet in the car park. The vet was lovely and she talked me though next steps. They would take Posh in to have a look at her and then talk through possible treatment options.

It only took five minutes before they called me back. They needed to do a couple of extra checks, but the initial feedback was exactly the same as Anna had given me. My heart was beginning to sink and I was barely keeping it together in front of Anna.

And then the vet came out and I could tell from her demeanour that this wasn't going to be good news. It did appear that Posh was suffering and we had a few options, although as it turned out, not great options. They could try to drain the fluids which would involve sedating her and making her thoroughly miserable again. This would also involve putting her on another course of tablets and Posh just hated taking her meds. With this option, the chances of the fluids filling up again were very high. We could carry on with the steroids and the diuretics with no great prospect of them clearing her condition. Or finally, we could decide to put Posh to sleep and to stop her suffering.

I was literally reeling by this time and it was then that Anna declared her hand. She told the vet that she was a close friend of Jules and me and had come to offer support. She also told them that she worked for the referral vets and completely agreed with the vets diagnosis and list of options.

However much I hated it, I now had two opinions that amounted to the same outcome. It was time for me to do the right thing and stop Posh's misery. Then again, I couldn't make that decision on my own. I had to sit down with Jules when she was home later that evening. I turned to Anna, who was shivering in the cold without a coat and I clearly saw a tear sliding down her cheek. And through my own tears, I told both vets that it was time to put Posh first. I just needed to speak to Jules before making our final decision.

It was then that Anna totally astounded me by offering to put Posh to sleep for us at home. We had always wanted this to be the case – in the warmth and love of their own home rather than in a soulless vet's surgery. It was the ultimate honour for Anna to offer to do this. Humbling.

The drive home with Anna and Posh was difficult and I think we both were too upset to really think about what had been decided. But Anna's offer had left me moved and emotional.

Jules told me later that when she was driving home that evening, she knew. She knew that I hadn't called her as agreed because the decision was the one she didn't want to hear. She had a feeling that our lives were about to change forever.

When she arrived I poured her the biggest drink possible and started to tell the story. We were broken and devastated. They were our kids and only two years after we had experienced the same situation with Becks - we were here again.

We initially asked Anna to come round on the Monday night, but then changed our minds. We wanted one full extra day with our darling. As it turned out this was a perfect decision as were able to spend Tuesday in the garden with HRH Posh. She loved the weak February sun and we hugged her like our lives depended on it. The awful passing of the hours until the evening was the only thing on our mind. I had my fair share of doubts about what we had decided. Posh was after all eating and drinking well, but her spirit had gone and she looked tired all the time. We never did get to hear that gorgeous purr once more.

Worse still, she would never show that feisty side again or so we thought.

Anna and her husband Chris (also a super vet) arrived in the evening and handled the whole thing with incredible sensitivity and compassion. They talked us through the options again and all four of us again said this was for the best for Posh.

Posh passed to the Rainbow Bridge early that evening. We were able to hold her and tell her how much we loved her right to the end. Amazingly, that feisty side did come out one more time as she attempted to get to her litter – what dignity. We were told afterwards that she wouldn't have been aware of what she was doing, but we like to think that was Posh just being her best stroppy self. That's why we loved her.

We had prepared a satin lined box for Posh and included her favourite toys and photographs of us and her sister. We laid Posh out on the bed and brought Flo in to say her goodbye. She promptly jumped over Posh to explore the box – so Flo like!

The next evening, we took Posh to church and as we did with Becks, Jules played Nimrod for her.

The next night we buried our darling, next to her beloved sister.

Her memorial says:

HRH Posh

Forever in our hearts

See you and Becks at the Rainbow Bridge

Love Mum, Dad and Flo xxx

What we can't get used to is the silence. Posh walking around our bedroom, forever fidgeting and scraping at the litter in our bathroom. No one prepares you for this. The "Oracle" Katie said she felt the same when it happened to her.

Our friends, family and customers have been amazing since Posh attained her angel wings. We even received a lovely bouquet of flowers from Anna and Chris. Posh's godmother Ginny wrote some amazing words in her card saying, 'She was honoured to know her, to be her friend and her godmother, thank you for that privilege'. Totally beautiful words.

Other friends came out with inspirational statements such as, 'We go through the heartaches with our babies, so that they don't have to. This beautiful angel needs to fly'.

So instead of finishing the book on a full stop, I'd like to finish with some hope.

What if this isn't the end?

What if there is a Rainbow Bridge?

What if all our beloved pets are waiting for us?

Maybe they come back to reassure us that they're still around. We've certainly had a few signals from Posh in the last couple of weeks, such as hearing her footsteps in our bedroom or a shadow we can't quite explain. Even Flo has got in on the act, eating Posh's favourite foods and staring at empty space in the hallway. Could it be Posh she sees?

Maybe the robins on Posh's memorial, really are trying to tell us that everything is alright. And that Snowy, Michelle, Blackie, Bob, Posh and Becks have found each other. Free of pain and restored to their youth.

So it's not the end of something.

It's a beginning.

I've chosen to finish on a happy note, however much my heart is aching.

Two weeks later, Jules and I walked down the end of the garden on St Beck's Day (14 February) and read each other cards from Posh and Becks. We toasted them with Champagne and we suddenly felt at peace. They were finally playing together at the Rainbow Bridge.

Wherever we go, whatever we do - Posh and Becks will always be in our hearts.

EPILOGUE

Confession time

In our kitchen we have a plaque on the wall which says, 'Life's journey to the grave isn't about arriving safe and sound, but skidding in sideways screaming, what a ride!'. This seems to sum up the way that Jules and me have led our lives.

It's been a rollercoaster of experiences and emotions. I'm sure that my life wouldn't have been as much fun without my feline friends coming along for the ride.

Some of the names in the book have been changed to protect the innocent (and the guilty) – the latter know who they are! Even some of the cat names have been changed for exactly the same reason.

Confession time! Every single word in the book is true with the one exception of the whole of Chapter 20.

When I started writing the book (February 2020), we were booked to travel to Nepal at the end of the year. We were planning on paying our tribute to the miracle cat – Becks. Then Covid-19 came along followed by a long period of lockdown in the UK and right across the world. Our holiday was already booked, but we had to cancel it.

We *will* travel to Base Camp and we *will* place Becks' cat nip mouse at the foot of Everest. But we won't be doing that for a couple of years.

So I wrote the chapter as if it had really happened. Older readers will remember when a whole series of the TV show Dallas was explained away as a dream sequence. The character Bobby, instead of dying had gone into the shower and dreamt what had happened. Only to emerge five minutes later and the world was just the same. Well Chapter 20 is "my Dallas".

I hope you don't feel cheated by this, but the book needed an ending and the miracle cat needed her tribute. Chapter 20 was due to be the end of the book. But then Flo came along and Posh was determined to have the final word.

Rest in peace Princess Becks and HRH Posh xx

The Rainbow Bridge

There is a bridge connecting Heaven and Earth.
It is called the Rainbow Bridge because of all its
beautiful colours.
Just this side of the Rainbow Bridge there is a land of
meadows, hills and valleys with lush green grass.
When a beloved pet dies, the pet goes to this place.
There is always food and water and warm spring weather.
The old and frail animals are young again.
Those who were sick, hurt or in pain are made
whole again.
There is only one thing missing, they are not with their
special person who loved them so much on earth.
So each day they run and play until the day comes when
one suddenly stops playing and looks up!
The nose twitches! The ears are up!
The eyes are staring and this one runs from the group!
You have been seen and when you and your special
friend meet, you take him in your arms and hug him.
He licks and kisses your face again and again -and you
look once more into the eyes of your best friend and
trusting pet.
Then you cross the Rainbow Bridge together never again
to be apart.

Author: unknown

Printed in Great Britain
by Amazon